WHOLENESS IN WORSHIP

WHOLENESS
IN WORSHIP

Thomas Neufer Emswiler

Sharon Neufer Emswiler

HARPER & ROW, PUBLISHERS

SAN FRANCISCO

Cambridge
Hagerstown
Philadelphia
New York

1817

London
Mexico City
São Paulo
Sydney

FIRST EDITION

Designer: Jim Mennick

Library of Congress Cataloging in Publication Data

Neufer Emswiler, Thomas
  WHOLENESS IN WORSHIP.

  Filmography: p. 00
  Bibliography: p. 00
  1. Public worship. I. Neufer Emswiler, Sharon, joint author. II. Title.
BV15.N49 1980   264   79–2982
ISBN 0–06–062247–4

80 81 82 83 84 10 9 8 7 6 5 4 3 2 1

Contents

Introduction

WE HAVE had enough fragmentation. For too long we have been fractured into puzzle pieces. In order to be mended physically we have had to seek out an appropriate specialist for the particular part that seems to have gone wrong. Educationally we have been pushed into perfecting only one small part, our conscious mind, in what has often become a trivialization of our energies to meet certain degree requirements. In religion most of us have long been forced to worship in ways that do not recognize our physical bodies. We have been conditioned to accept this as the "norm" for "good" worship. We have also been encouraged to segregate ourselves in worship from those who are different, especially from the very young and those of other racial backgrounds.

We have been taught that things are either good or bad, right or wrong, correct or incorrect. Matthew Fox in *Whee! We, Wee All the Way Home*[1] points out that one doesn't have to believe in astrology to see the significance of the name of the age from which we are just emerging—Pisces, symbolized by two fish swimming in opposite directions. What better symbol for the "either-or" fragmentation we have been experiencing? According to astrologists, the age into which we are going is Aquarius, symbolized by the water bearer, who represents the deep, the source from which all life comes. The contrasting symbolism expresses movement from "either-or" to "both-and."

Though change comes slowly, it is relentless. It has occurred most dramatically in the health care fields. Specialized, sometimes almost to absurdity, more and more doctors, nurses, psychiatrists, and social workers are attempting to reintroduce wholism in medical treatment and prevention. They are recognizing how intricately connected are the mind, body, and spirit, and realizing that treatment of an isolated malady may be almost useless if that treatment is not linked with care for the whole person.

Change in education seems slower, but a number of educational institutions are changing their degree requirements to allow for more general approaches to learning. New degrees are gaining popularity, especially in areas such as the ministry, where practical experience and understanding are prized. Many schools of theology now offer a Doctor of Ministry degree for those interested in improving their practical skills. Even in those areas where specialization is still crucial, students are being encouraged to take a more comprehensive approach in their undergraduate education and to see the interconnectedness of their specialty with other fields.

Christians are also responding to the concern for wholeness in worship. In ancient times worshipers demonstrated that the whole person (mind, body, spirit) must be involved in experiences celebrating ultimate concerns, but this knowledge became blurred and almost faded in the struggles of the centuries. Today a restless yearning is present, especially among the laity, for something more than the traditional mainline Protestant or Catholic service. The startling emergence of the charismatic movement within mainline denominations is in part a reflection of this yearning. The charismatics know we have bodies. They aren't afraid to use them in worship, and they aren't afraid to claim body-related gifts such as healing. Some people are willing to swallow a rigid and sometimes simplistic theology in their hunger for what they call "alive" worship. The resurgence of interest in and practice of meditation in various forms also reflects a need for something not generally met through mainline worship services. Such services may originally have been developed for growth of the inner life of the spirit, but their present liturgical style works against such growth.

Although signs of a new worship style are appearing, as far as we know no one has yet attempted to integrate a comprehensive description of this new style with a theoretical explanation of why it is developing. What is needed is a resource that gives insight into how worship may be designed to reflect current understandings of wholism and yet also maintain historical and theological validity. For the past couple of years, we have been working on this task. What follows in this book is by no means a completed product. We don't expect such completion from ourselves or anyone else. The nature of this enterprise does not allow absolute answers; it encourages tentative probings, gentle suggestions: that's what this book is. It is informed especially by our study of feminist theology and of inclusive language, both of which have led us to new understandings of wholeness. It is also influenced by a serious quest into the psychology that stems from the Swiss psychologist C. G. Jung and what it says about us as humans. Jungian psychology has led us in turn to other psychological approaches that stress in one way or another the essential unity of mind, body, and spirit. We have also discovered that the concept of wholeness in worship is not brand new but is rooted in basic biblical understandings, foremost among them the concept of *shalom* (wholeness, maturity, peace).

In this book we provide a basic definition of wholistic worship that includes both a theological grounding and more detailed reflections on insights gained through feminist and liberation theologians and through the insights of wholistic health. We then look at some of the specific aspects of wholistic worship (part by part as it were) beginning with mind/body/spirit integration and its implications for worship and flowing from there into a discussion of inclusive language, ages, cultures, and religious traditions. We discuss the pastoral focus of wholistic worship—concern for the handicapped (which includes all of us) and the mission thrust of wholistic worship (concern for the whole world). We discuss the significance of the arts and the use of our senses in wholistic worship. We look at the importance of valuing all our times in wholistic worship

—past, present, and future; good, blah, and bad. We share how wholistic worship affirms both traditional parts of a service—word *and* table. We examine the ways in which wholistic worship gives us new insights into the special services of baptisms, weddings, healings, and funerals. The final chapter gives examples of wholistic worship services in which we have shared.

In a sense a book on wholistic worship is something of a contradiction. It is naturally more linear and rational than a face-to-face encounter. It involves some dissecting and fragmenting in an attempt to bring about greater clarity. Our hope, however, is that this book will reveal at least part of the essence of what we have discovered as wholistic worship. In this attempt we will be frankly personal at points, sharing the joys and frustrations of our own practical experiences.

Both of us are ordained United Methodist ministers. We have served in both large and small local churches before coming to our present positions in campus ministry at Illinois State University in Normal, Illinois. As co-directors of the Wesley Foundation at this university we have found more opportunity for and challenge in worship than even in our local churches. We have two services each week. One takes place on Sunday morning in the University Union. A student committee often helps in developing and carrying out this service. The other happens each Wednesday evening in the sanctuary of the First United Methodist Church, which is located right at the edge of the campus. This communion service is held at 9:30 P.M., to fit in with student schedules.

Several years ago we wrote a book sharing our concern for the use of inclusive language in worship. Called *Women and Worship: A Guide to Non-Sexist Hymns, Prayers, and Liturgies,*[2] this book was fairly widely read and resulted in our being invited to lead workshops many places about the country. We also used some of the thoughts in this book in editing a hymnal entitled *Sisters and Brothers, Sing!*[3] This has already been reprinted and seems to be meeting a real need within the church.

We spent the first five months of 1978 on sabbatical. Half of that time we were in Evanston, Illinois, reading, experiencing workshops, and teaching a course at Garrett-Evangelical Theological Seminary called "Worship from a Feminist Perspective." The second half of our sabbatical was spent in Denver, studying at The Center for New Beginnings (Jungian work particularly) and teaching the same course at Iliff School of Theology. The opportunity to share many of our ideas in a teaching situation among sensitive, intelligent students was invaluable in developing the material in this book. As we taught the course, we discovered that much that we had labeled as feminist worship could also be called wholistic. We had approached wholism through the feminist door.

One other important fact about us: we are the parents of a five-year-old and an infant. They have taught us much about the body, spontaneity, and enjoyment. They have also helped us to see more clearly how much most worship services are really for "adults only."

This book is a combination then of intensive study and reading we have been doing for years in the area of worship, together with our experiences of leading worship services and workshops in many different settings and teaching worship courses in seminaries. We have stated our ideas strongly at points because they come from deep conviction forged from many experiences. At the same time, however, we approach the task of writing this book in fear and trembling. We know we are by no means "expert" enough to be right all the time. We know we carry prejudices and blindness into our writing just as others do whom we may be quick to criticize. We ask, therefore, that you read this book with a heart open to our humanness. Accept what rings true in your own heart and ponder the rest, recognizing that your insight and experience is also valuable and valid. Among us all rests the spirit of truth who will help each of us move ever more surely to the center of real worship. With such help, how can we lose?

1

What Is Wholeness in Worship?

BASIC DEFINITION

Wholeness in worship is expressed through the disciplined coming together of Christians to celebrate with their whole beings—body, mind, and spirit—the God who brings meaning, unity, and fulfillment to their lives. Persons involved in wholistic worship are committed to the Old Testament promise of shalom and to the New Testament possibility of the peace of Christ. They realize that wholeness is embodied in action as well as ritual. It is a preview, as it were, of the Messianic banquet; the fulfillment of God's reign.

The person who worships wholistically understands the need for both private and public experiences of worship. Private worship is necessary for the sensitive development of the individual's inner life. Public worship is necessary for the sharing of diverse gifts of community, so that each person is enriched by the others. To achieve real wholeness in worship individuals must be involved in the disciplined coming-together of a community of Christians. As Paul pointed out in 1 Corinthians 12, separately we are but parts of the body; together we *are* the body.

To celebrate the God who brings our lives meaning, unity, and fulfillment means for the Christian first of all to celebrate

God's love as revealed in Jesus Christ for all humanity. The truth of God as discovered in Christ therefore becomes our focal point. From that flow all other celebrations of meaning, unity, and fulfillment. Thus the community in wholistic worship not only celebrates God's love for them and for the whole world, but they also celebrate the love they know for one another, the beauty of a butterfly and of the whole universe, the powerful truth found in other traditions, even the non-Christian, the creative potential of science, and the awe of great art. All things that point toward human meaning, unity, and fulfillment are appropriate for worship celebration. Conversely, the community that worships wholistically must grieve over that which prevents meaning, unity, and fulfillment. They must look with stark realism at the destructive powers at loose in the universe and in each of us. Confessing this reality and asking God's help in confronting it are crucial to wholeness in worship.

THEOLOGICAL UNDERPINNINGS

Many key Christian words found in worship come from the same roots as the word *whole.* The words *holy* and *whole* share the same root formation.[1] That which is truly holy is that which is moving toward wholeness. The word *salvation* comes from the same root as the word *salve.* One valid description of the meaning of salvation is that which brings healing and wholeness. Although the Hebrew word *shalom* is usually translated as "peace," "wholeness" or "fulfillment" would be a better translation. The concept of shalom is a major Old Testament theme that continues in the New Testament in its identification with the concept of *eirēnē,* which is also often translated "peace." Both *eirēnē* and *shalom* have many layers of meaning that cannot be represented by a single-word translation.[2] The best short summary of the concept of shalom that we have found is in the book *The Church for Others.*

> This word (*shalom*) is used to indicate all aspects of human life in its full and God-given maturity; righteousness, truth, fellowship,

peace, etc. This single word summarizes all the gifts of the messianic age; even the name of the Messiah can simply be *shalom* (Micah 5:5; Eph. 2:4); the Gospel is a Gospel of *shalom* (Eph. 6:15), and the God proclaimed in this Gospel can often be called the God of *shalom. Shalom* is not something that can be objectified and set apart. It is not the plus which the haves can distribute to the have-nots, nor is it an internal condition (peace of mind) that some can enjoy in isolation. *Shalom* is a social happening, an event in interpersonal relations. It can therefore never be reduced to a simple formula; it has to be discovered as God's gift in actual situations.[3]

The inner dynamic of shalom is outward in concern for the world. Once the truth of shalom touches us, we know that this truth can only find fulfillment as all people are included. This dynamic is at work in the Bible. The later Old Testament prophets knew that Israel's mission was to be "a light to the gentiles." The gift of shalom could not be hoarded; it had to be shared. The same truth came to the New Testament Christians as they debated whether or not the faith should be open unconditionally to non-Jews. Part of the inner essence of shalom seems to be inclusiveness.

The same driving force is present in wholistic worship. It is not satisfied until all are one in God. Excluding people because of their age, race, cultural background, physical or mental handicaps, or religious tradition is a denial of shalom and precludes wholeness in worship. The same is true of more subtle exclusions in worship such as the use of sexist language and overemphasizing the mind at the expense of the body. Wholistic worship also insists on the valuing of all our times, past, present, and future. It knows that worship which rests in any of these periods exclusively is fractured. Wholeness in worship moves us toward social commitment. We celebrate our journey toward personal fulfillment but recognize that this journey is inevitably thwarted unless we also move toward social fulfillment. The problems of our world must become our individual problems in order for shalom to have real integrity.

The concept of shalom was best expressed by Jesus at two

key points in his ministry. In the Sermon on the Mount, one whole section of Jesus' teaching is climaxed by the command, "Be perfect, therefore, as your heavenly Father is perfect" (Matt. 5:48, NIV). A better rendering of the meaning of this passage is "be whole as God is whole." Jesus was not talking about unattainable moral or physical attributes, which only God could have, but about the kind of maturity, or wholeness, toward which most of us strive and which is fully possible were we to live in accord with the radical claims of Jesus' teaching in the Sermon on the Mount.

Jesus poignantly expressed his own deep longing for the wholeness of the world in his prayer that all Christians may be one as Jesus and God are one (see John 17:21). Although especially directed to believers and those who accept the faith because of the first believers, this prayer harkens back to John 3:16 and the salvation gift of Jesus for the whole world. Whenever we celebrate shalom, we look toward the actualization of Jesus' prayer.

INSIGHTS FROM FEMINIST THEOLOGY

One of the doors through which we came to many of our understandings of wholeness in worship is feminist theology. Although a comprehensive description of feminist theology is not possible in this book, some basic definitions are important. First, the word *feminist* does not mean someone interested only in women or someone who believes women are superior and should rule the world. A feminist is committed to the belief that women and men should be treated equally and is dedicated to actively furthering this belief. A feminist advocates and practices treating women and men as human persons and willingly contravenes social customs when to do so is necessary.

Both men and women can be feminists, an idea convincingly demonstrated by Leonard Swidler in his now classic article, "Jesus Was a Feminist."[4] Feminist theology is based on a concern for treating all persons as human beings. Because of the sexist nature of our society, in feminist theology special attention is given to women and to their unique gifts and insights. Because it is especially concerned about the oppression of women, feminist theology is by nature liberation theology. The concern for the freedom of all peoples is seen through the particular experiences of women, but an affinity with other liberation theologies is inevitable, whether they be those of blacks, Third World peoples, or gay persons.[5]

Theology has long been the domain of male writers and teachers (primarily white, first-world males), who have tended to overemphasize certain aspects of theology and neglect or ignore others. Feminist theology seeks to bring a new balance to theological perspective, but because the emphasis of theology has for so long been on what are called patriarchal values and ways of thinking, feminist theology feels driven at this point to emphasize the opposite. Patriarchal values, often identified with the male, are not inherently masculine, and feminist values, often identified with females, are not inherently feminine. What feminism and wholism finally long for is a balance between these values, celebrating and using the best in both.

A key insight of feminism has been its espousal of the concept of androgyny[6] (*andro,* "male"; *gyny,* "female"). Through his study of the human psyche, C. G. Jung showed the psychological truth that all of us are a combination of what we have traditionally called masculine and feminine traits. Our culture has generally steered us into affirming one set of traits at the expense of the other, but in a whole person the masculine and feminine are balanced. Such a balance brings wholeness and health. Because of our cultural pressures, this means that men usually need to work much more on traditionally feminine traits and women on the traditionally masculine traits. The final goal, however, is androgyny, a blending of both feminine and masculine.

Feminist theology contrasts with most traditional theology in several ways. Feminist theology emphasizes the *subjective, intuitive* approach to truth, and most traditional theology emphasizes the objective, rational approach. Feminist theology does not maintain that rationality is of no value but that it has limits. Other ways of reaching truth are also valid. Feminists point out that feeling and intuition are important means of knowing God. "Feeling" religion can of course degenerate into mindless fanaticism, but it can be a vital antidote to the sterile rationalism that can kill the spirit. When feelings are valued in worship, services are warm and emotional rather than cool and rational. Fantasy and imagination are stimulated, and time is allowed for silence, reflection, and meditation. Rational concerns are not neglected, but a warmer, more human element is added that is often missing from many mainline worship services.

We have visited worship services of many different denominations around the country and have found that most are overbalanced either toward the rational or toward the feeling. In almost every case, those services in which genuine feelings were emphasized seemed to occur in alive and growing churches. Those churches that emphasized the rational in their services were often struggling just to maintain themselves. Some growing churches, however, did emphasize rationality in their services, but they compensated for their lack of emphasis on feelings in worship by recognizing them in other ways, for example, through adult Sunday school classes in which personal love and concern were primary. The problem with many services in which feelings were emphasized was that solid theology was in short supply. The congregations were asked, either implicitly or explicitly, to accept simplistic concepts of faith that made no sense. What was needed was balance.

Feminist theology also values the inductive rather than the deductive and emphasizes the concrete rather than the abstract. The arts have been an important aspect of worship because they approach reality from the concrete. For example, they help us discover the truth about love by showing someone in love, not by giving a philosophical definition of love. The art of storytelling has always been used in worship. Jesus used it almost exclusively. Any minister worth his or her salt today knows the importance of storytelling, and many ministers even complain that the only thing people remember about their sermons is the stories. And maybe that's the best thing for them to remember. Abstract generalizations tend to lack life and remain tied to our minds. Stories tend to make us grapple with ourselves and with the issues. They reappear in our consciousness to teach us when we need them.

Several years ago we heard a sermon about the importance of making our love real in compassionate, concrete actions. The details of the sermon have long since faded, but we still remember vividly the central story of the sermon, which contained its essence beautifully.

A university professor, who was an internationally known expert in child psychology, had written a number of best-selling books on the subject and had spoken at workshops and conferences all over the world. He was also a builder and designer in his spare time and with his wife had designed and built their own house.

After several years of painstaking labor, the house was finally completed, and all that remained to be done was the concrete walks. The professor spent an entire day mixing and pouring concrete. Exhausted but finally done, he was in his house resting contentedly when suddenly he heard strange sounds outside. He ran to the window just in time to see some neighborhood youngsters running through his freshly poured concrete. Of course, he was furious. He recognized some of the children as belonging next door and so went there to complain. The mother of the family opened the door, and the professor proceeded to unload. He was so angry he could hardly speak but finally got out why he was so upset.

Naturally the mother was concerned and sorry that her children had been part of such an act, but at the same time she couldn't help but be amused by the professor's manner. She had never seen him so upset. Finally when he stopped sputtering, she looked at him with a twinkle in her eye and said: "Professor, I'm sorry for what my children did, but I can't help but be surprised by your anger. I've read several of your books, and I know that you make the point in them again and again that we are to love our children. Now, professor, don't you love these children?"

The professor drew himself up to his full height, looked the woman in the eye, and said, "Madam, I only love children in the abstract, not in the concrete."

Feminist theology values relational understandings of reality and recognizes that theology which does not help to inform our everyday life is virtually meaningless. It recognizes too that the primary way of discovering and experiencing the truth of God's love is through relationships, both human and divine. Traditional theology, on the other hand, has often been so concerned with "universal" significance that it has not attempted to get specific. It has developed systematic explanations of sin and forgiveness without ever helping people see how these concepts impinge on their common life. When a congregation takes relationships seriously , they will strive to find ways to increase the participatory quality of worship. The congregation takes relationships seriously, they will strive to find ways to increase the participatory quality of worship. The cepts to the experiences of her or his congregation and will encourage them to share together as friends at times other than formal worship. They will also be given an opportunity in worship for greetings, touch, song, and movement. They will be challenged to continue the incarnation (by having Christ live in them) as they relate to one another during the week.

Feminist theology is also much more circular than linear in its approach to communication. For a long time, emphasis has been on the word, actually on the written word. Services have been orderly; one thing has followed another according to a carefully printed bulletin. It was not always so. Before the invention of the printing press (and still today in the Eastern tradition and in black and Hispanic services) worship was much less regulated. Singing, praying, and preaching all occurred simultaneously. Spontaneity was allowed and encouraged. Services didn't necessarily begin at 11 A.M. and end exactly one hour later; a service might last half a day. Most of us are probably not eager to stay for four- and five-hour services, but we might be inspired by a little less order and a little more spontaneity and surprise.

Feminist theology is also communal rather than hierarchical. One reason feminist theology has produced no "giants" such as Paul Tillich or Karl Barth is that it is much more committed to the possibility of a community working out theological concepts rather than one superstar doing all the work. Groups of women share at conferences such as Grailville.[7] This group approach also has implications for worship. Rather than worship being the work of the minister, passively shared and participated in by the congregation, feminist theology wants it to be again "the work of the people," facilitated and enabled by a professional minister. The people need to be significantly involved in the planning of worship through a committee or some other structure. Services that maximize participation by the whole worshiping community include, for example, sermon talk-backs, lay liturgists, and the sharing of joys and concerns.

Feminist theology is inclusive rather than exclusive in its orientation. Feminist theology always asks, Who is left out? If inclusiveness is a primary concern in worship, the use of worshiping practices from any and all denominations can be considered, as can the use of practices from other religions or from secular sources. The physical setting for worship will be designed to assure that people are not left out, and both verbal and nonverbal inclusive language will be used. A concern for inclusiveness will result in a style of worship that is not structured in ways that completely leave out children, old people, or persons of a particular ethnic background.

Feminist theology also emphasizes *praxis,* the action-reflection model. Merely talking about an issue is never enough; talk must be informed and transformed by action. On the other hand, action without careful reflection is often hasty and ineffective. Therefore, reflection is as important as action. This means that worship cannot be satisfied to be only a dramatic rehearsal of God's love for the world. Mission is an essential part of worship, reflected especially in a time of offering and dedication. These times must be more than talk; they need to impel toward action.

Finally, feminist theology is process oriented. It recognizes that truth is a changing reality and that no single theology ever captures all the truth for all time. It knows the value of being open to change even within itself. This means that no form or content of worship is absolute. We must always be open to the leadings of the Spirit to develop new possibilities.

The chart that follows summarizes our discussion of feminist theology and its implications for worship. The dichotomies are not generally either-or choices but are both-and possibilities. To bring balance back to worship, emphases of feminist theology will have to be vigorously proposed, but not at the expense of other valuable traditional concepts. We are struggling toward a model of wholeness in worship that affirms, values, and uses all the divergent parts.

Feminist Theology and Worship — Putting the Two Together

Feminist theology is characterized by the following descriptive phrases:	Implications for Worship
1. Emphasis on the SUBJECTIVE, INTUITIVE (FEELING); rather than objective, rational thinking).	Emphasizes warm and emotional services rather than cool and rational. Use of fantasy and imagination. Time for silence, reflection, meditation.
2. INDUCTIVE rather than deductive; emphasis on the CONCRETE.	Serious concern for use of the arts in worship.
3. RELATIONAL: concerned about everyday life experiences and how they relate to theology and vice-versa.	Emphasis upon participatory worship with the congregation sharing in joys and concerns, greetings, touch, song, etc.
4. CIRCULAR rather than linear.	Open to multimedia experiences in worship. Less emphasis on printed bulletin. Possibilities for spontaneity carefully planned into the service.

5. COMMUNAL rather than hierarchical.	Planning of services by worship committee rather than by pastor alone. Services planned in such a way as to maximize participation by the whole worshipping community (sermon talk-back, lay liturgists, prayers written by laity).
6. INCLUSIVE rather than exclusive ("both and" rather than "either or").	Open to using meaningful worshipping practices from all denominations, other religions, and secular sources. Careful to be inclusive in use of language, both verbal and nonverbal.
7. PRAXIS: action/reflection model (Justice out of oppression).	Sees mission as an essential part of worship, reflected especially in the offering and dedication parts of worship.
8. PROCESS oriented.	Sees no form or content of worship as absolute, and is thus open to the leadings of the Spirit to develop new possibilities for worship in each moment.

INSIGHTS GAINED FROM WHOLISTIC HEALTH

A revolution is happening in our midst. Because it is fairly quiet, many are unaware of it or only vaguely sense its significance. Because it has no central coordinating group and no particular location, it is hard to pin down. Its effects are felt in the rising popularity of all kinds of alternatives to traditional medicine, including high-level wellness, acupuncture, spiritual healing, and biofeedback. Traditional medicine has usually treated symptoms by means of chemicals (prescriptions) or surgery. Many of the new health-care systems treat the whole person—body, mind, and spirit. Many are also studying energy-flow as a resource for healing and wellness. So little is

known about the energy forces we generate that much of this
work is nonscientific, but enough data is being collected to
indicate that some kind of energy-flow exists in people and that
it can be used in a positive way.[8]

Many traditional physicians have attempted to discount
these alternative systems, and they have been instrumental in
getting many states to pass restrictive laws to prevent people
from practicing healing (medicine) without a license. Some of
what is happening in wholistic health today is quackery, but
not all of it. The number of valid and scientifically documented
healings that have occurred through unorthodox methods have
caused many doctors to look seriously at the movement to see
what they can learn. They have formed their own physicians
group concerned with wholistic health.[9] Some have been referring patients who seem incurable to Dr. Carl Simonton and
Stephanie Mathews-Simonton, who operate the Cancer Counseling and Research Center, for their unique treatment involving imagery.[10] Many have also taken a second look at spiritual
healing and have become involved in working with someone
who does this work, such as Father Francis MacNutt.[11]

In addition to being a fascinating and significant field in
itself, wholistic health has contributions to make to worship.
First and most important, it is underlining the interconnection
between mind and body. Mind cannot be separated from body,
either in living or in worship, and yet most mainline churches
have structured worship services as if we humans were practi-
cally bodiless. Other than those body parts used in standing up
and sitting down, the only part of the body we use in worship
is the head. If we are concerned with touching the depths of our
souls, we must learn to make use of all that we are—body,
mind, and spirit. If we are to present our bodies as a living
sacrifice before God (see Rom. 12:2), then we are called to use
our whole beings in our worship.

The wholistic health revolution also calls us to a new awareness of and concern for the role of healing in worship. From the
beginning of Christianity, healing services were a part of many

worshiping communities. In our own time, however, they have fallen into disrepute. Because we have surrendered this area to radio and TV evangelists who are often not responsible in either their methods or their claims, we have lost an important dimension in our worship. Wholistic worship seeks to find ways to recover the power of healing (both physical and mental) as a part of worship that maintains historical and rational respectability. If responsible Christians do not enter this area, it will continue to be a source of pain and division. Developed carefully it can be a source of tremendous promise and power.

2

Mind-Body-Spirit Integration and the Implications for Worship

WE HAVE been alluding to the importance of mind-body-spirit integration as a basic part of wholistic health. This integration has special significance in four areas—rhythm, movement, touch, and silence. These are not the only areas affected, but they are the most significant for worship. In this chapter we introduce some insights concerning the relationship of each to mind-body-spirit integration; these insights are then developed in later chapters as we deal with other parts of the circle that encompasses wholistic worship.

RHYTHM

In the second half of the seventeenth century Christian Huygens, a Dutch scientist, noticed that two pendulum clocks mounted beside each other on a wall would swing together in precise rhythm. They would hold their mutual beat far beyond their capacity to be matched in mechanical accuracy. It seemed as if they "wanted" to keep the same time. Huygens assumed a kind of "sympathy" between them and experimented to learn just how the interaction took place. He discovered that the pendulums were synchronized by a slight impulse through the wall and thus explained for the first time what scientists now call "mutual phase-locking of two oscillators," or "entrainment."

This phenomenon is now known to be universal. Whenever two or more oscillators in the same field are pulsing at nearly the same time, they tend to "lock in" so that they are pulsing at exactly the same time. Nature searches for the most efficient energy state, and less energy is required to pulse in cooperation than in opposition.

This fact about oscillators has implications for mind-body-spirit integration. If our minds and bodies are inextricably interrelated, could we not also be bound to the whole universe? Could we be part of some cosmic rhythm? Could discovering the meaning of life be somehow tied to being able to flow with this rhythm rather than opposing it?

If these questions seem far out to you, consider some facts from your own experience. You know, for example, how external circumstances can affect your internal attitude. A cloudy day may bring intense depression and melancholy; a sunny day fairly shouts away the blues. Studies have shown that the composition of human blood alters in relation to sunspot cycles.[1] Some people seem to energize us, and others seem to drain energy from us. Could all these examples relate to the basic life force rhythmically at work throughout the universe?

Meditators in all the great religions have talked of becoming one with the universe, of somehow getting into the cosmic rhythm and flowing with it. The rhythm of the chanted "OM" of Hinduism, Sikhism, and Lamaism and the reverberating bells of Buddhism have long been claimed to be tied to the pulsing rhythm at the heart of the universe. This rhythm is also reflected in the heartbeat of humans and animals. Although our heartbeats may not be in entrainment, they are a part of the pulsing vibrancy at the center of life. Much of the power of music lies in rhythms, which, no matter how varied, are related to the basic beat of life.

In the past, it has usually been accidental for worship to be synchronized with the pulsing rhythms of the universe, but the impact on worshipers, when it occurred, was significant. Chants and music in worship reflect this rhythm, but other ways of connecting with the power of this rhythm may also exist. Seeing each human body as a hologram or complete expression of the universe may help us to become aware of new ways of experiencing ourselves, one another, and God. We can open ourselves to the beat within us and become aware of the powerful statement about the ongoingness of life our heart makes. We can also become sensitive to the pulse and heartbeat of others. Entrainment between two persons is almost magical. We need times in worship for listening to our own heart and for being in touch with the pulse of another. Becoming aware of the holy beat of life in us is also becoming aware of God. It is as if God were saying, "Here am I in the least of these" (see Matt. 25:40). Chapter 12 contains one sample of how this might be done.

The idea of using handclapping and other rhythm-producing media such as drums in worship is worth exploring more fully. When we worked at an American Indian vocational school a number of years ago, we learned about the importance of the drums to our Indian friends. Every evening about sundown the drums would begin calling the Indians together for dancing and sharing. These drums reflected the life-beat of the world; they were an energizing, encouraging force to tired and sometimes beaten-down people. It is impossible to transfer such a symbol across cultures, but perhaps persons of other cultures can discover ways to incorporate some of that power in their own ritual observances.

Great preachers have always known the power of rhythm. In many black churches the rhythm of the preacher is so pronounced that a combo could be put behind him or her. Black preachers often burst into song as part of their sermon. Again it is not possible for one culture just to copy another and find that it has meaning, but a better understanding of the power of rhythm and experimenting with it in preaching can be helpful to anyone who wants the spoken word to come across with maximum impact.

MOVEMENT

Rhythm and movement naturally go together. It is almost impossible to keep our bodies still when great musical rhythm surrounds us. The essential vibrating quality of rhythm implies movement, yet movement itself is also important.

If mind, body, and spirit are integrated, then what we do with our bodies is just as important as what we do with our minds. In most worship services, however, our minds do all the work. On the other hand, evangelists have long known that the best way to move people emotionally is to move them physically. They have thus insisted that people walk to the front as a physical confirmation of their desire to live a new life in Christ. Dancers know the power of movement to underline and highlight an understanding that is beyond words. If dance is understood as any kind of rhythmic movement, then almost every movement in worship can be seen as dance, from the lighting of the candles at the beginning of a service to the raised hands of the celebrant in benediction at the conclusion.

If you have responsibility for corporate worship, you will probably find a movement inventory of each service helpful. Every physical gesture should be named and analyzed: for example, being led to a seat by an usher, standing up to sing a hymn, finding a responsive reading in a hymnal. After you determine what movements are happening on the part of everyone involved in the service, ask if these movements underline the basic theme of that part of worship or work against it. For example, if you wish a section of the service to be quiet and meditative, it is probably counterproductive to ask the congregation to stand to sing a hymn. On the other hand, if you want people to feel exuberance and joy, you would not have them sit while singing. In fact, you could ask them to process around the sanctuary while singing.

Worship can be choreographed so that the whole congregation can begin to experience the service with their bodies. Even simple movements such as clasping the hands in prayer or lifting the hands in praise can make a tremendous impact. Such movements need to be initiated through gentle suggestion, for particularly at first not everyone will participate. If the option of movement continues to be presented, however, amazing things can happen.

TOUCH

Infants in institutional settings have been known to die or come close to death because they received little human touch. Such reports have convinced us of how crucial human touch is to the very young, but most of us seem to assume that we outgrow the need for touch. This assumption is beautifully questioned in Sidney Simon's book, *Caring, Touching, Feeling.*[2] Simon believes that all of us have a basic skin hunger much like our physical appetite. We need touch as much as we need food. When we don't get it, something inside us withers.

Of course, many people are unaware of their need for touch because they have always had it in abundance. Many others in our society, however, especially those who live alone, may go weeks without another human touch.

A minister in Louisiana, who had a number of widows in his congregation, many of whom lived alone, intentionally instituted occasions in his worship service that would provide human touch. He became aware that many of these women were touched by no one all week long and came to worship hungry for the caring touch of another human hand.

We have also found this need on our college campus. Many students are away from their families and do not date regularly; they may have little opportunity to touch others. Instituting some simple contact gestures in our worship services has provided them with needed physical touch.

Touch is an extremely sensitive issue. For many in our culture, it is closely tied to sexuality. We conducted what we thought was a fairly nonthreatening service utilizing touch in a seminary classroom about a year ago. Several persons later told us that they disliked the service because they felt we were using touch superficially. They said they preferred not to touch someone unless they had already established a close relationship with that person. Even to clasp hands or join in a simple embrace was too much for them. They were right; touch is a sacred and important part of who we are. It should not be treated superficially. But in refusing to touch any but those they already knew deeply, were these students not making a comment about the limited nature of their own love, which could only be shared with a select group?

Touch is the language of love. It is ironic that worship services celebrating the God of love often do not include any human touch. Touching is vital to deeply meaningful worship. It answers deep body hungers of which we may not even be aware. Without it, we are less human, less alive.

For many years we have had a short communion service every Wednesday evening at 9:30 P.M. for college students. We have been amazed at how many students have come to this late service through all kinds of weather. Part of its attraction may be our emphasis on touch. As we serve each person the elements, we consciously touch him or her. If we're serving the bread, we touch the person's hand as we give him or her a piece of the bread. We touch the person on the shoulder as we hold the cup for the bread to be dipped in. People say they leave this service energized. Part of the reason may be our intentional use of touch.

SILENCE

If you have attended a Quaker meeting, you know something of the power of silence. It would seem that being silent alone or with a group would be about the same, but again and again those who are silent with a group report a power they do not find in their solitary times of silence. This is a power most churches and denominations seem to have forgotten.

It is almost hopeless to go to most worship services in search

of silence. "A time for silent prayer" may be listed in the bulletin, but almost always organ music fills this interlude. Many
worship leaders seem to be afraid of silence. They seem to think
every moment must be filled with something. Perhaps they
have a right to be frightened by silence. It is a powerful medium. It is also a threatening one.

Silence is ambiguous. It can be nothing or everything. Each
person can make of it what she or he wills. This very ambiguity
may be what scares most people. They are afraid to trust themselves or others to such a potentially vague experience.

The great saints throughout history clearly understood the
importance of silence. Our society, by its obsession to blot out
silence, also emphasizes its importance. Our bodies and our
minds need quiet. We are constantly bombarded by noise. If
worship is to renew and refresh us, silence is essential. In the
silence of both mind and body we are most likely to hear God's
voice. Without it, we might as well erect a brick wall.

Most of us are not prepared for a steady diet of absolute
silence, such as the Quakers sometimes practice. Instead, we
need periods of silence in the midst of other experiences. Times
of silence gain their real strength and power from the context
of what has gone before them and what may follow. In these
times we can direct one another out of pure ambiguity into
mutual meditation and prayer. In a later chapter we will share
ideas about how to use silence in worship. At this point, we
simply invite you to spend a few minutes quietly resting in
God.

3

The Importance of Language

LONG BEFORE we could provide the necessary facts and theories, we felt that language was as crucial in worship as it is in life. Sharon understood this first. Her account of how she was sickened by male dominated language is told in *Women and Worship*. After years of study, we can now also present theological, sociological, and psychological data to support our original conclusion based on feelings.

THEOLOGICAL UNDERPINNINGS

The Bible is often called the Word of God. Actually this is a misnomer. Jesus Christ is the Word; the Bible is words telling about events leading up to and developing after the coming of the Word. Still, for our purposes, the point is the same. The Christian faith has always been concerned with communication. The whole Bible, and certainly the Jesus event, can be seen as God's attempt to communicate with us. It is interesting too, that "The Word" metaphor has been seen as a central way of describing this struggle.

In his ministry, Jesus took the power of words with utmost seriousness. In the Sermon on the Mount, he spoke about the importance of saying a simple yes or no in making agreements, rather than going through the rigamarole of fancy oaths (see

Matt. 5:33 ff.). He also pointed out that it is important not to
heap up empty phrases in prayer but simply to say what you
really mean (see Matt. 6:7). Jesus' most forceful and striking
reference to the power of language came in his battle with the
scribes and the Pharisees. He was especially angered by their
hypocrisy and said:

> You brood of vipers! How can you speak good when you are evil?
> For out of the abundance of the heart the mouth speaks. The good
> person out of his or her treasure brings forth good, and the evil
> person out of his or her evil treasure brings forth evil. I tell you,
> on the day of judgment people will render account for every care-
> less word they utter; for *by your words you will be judged, and by
> your words you will be condemned* [Matt. 12:34–37; italics ours;
> paraphrase ours].

Concern for language was at the heart of the founding of the
church and the maintaining of it. The Tower of Babel story in
the Old Testament is a parable par excellence of how language
can fragment a people (see Gen. 11:1–9). Scholars have pointed
out that Pentecost (see Acts 2) was really a reversal of the Tower
of Babel. People came together who spoke many different languages, and somehow through the power of the gospel, they
understood as one. The Word was made clear to them. The
church therefore should be the agent to bring clarity out of
chaos. Through God's love, as shared in the church, we can all
understand one another again. That's the ideal; of course, we
don't need to emphasize how far short of this goal we are in
actual practice.

As the church developed, the importance of language as a
powerful means of communication continued. The "speaking in
tongues" controversy that occupied Paul (see 1 Cor. 14:6 ff.)
was basically a concern for clarity in communication. Paul
didn't condemn "speaking in tongues" outright. He merely said
that if it were done in public worship then it should be done
with some sense of order and propriety and that someone
should be available to interpret for the whole congregation.
Without this interpreter, Pentecost turns back into Babel.

As the early followers of Christ began to write down their experiences to share with others, they again struggled with communication. Lexographer Walter Bauer, in the introduction to his Greek lexicon, tells how the early New Testament writers developed new word formations, compounded old words with new, adopted foreign words, used specialized and technical terms and shifts in grammatical structure all in their attempts to communicate more clearly and forcefully. David Randolph, writer, minister, and worship resource person, in commenting on Bauer's article says, "If Koine Greek at last became sublime, it was not without these agonizing linguistic adventures in which the first Christians participated and which the New Testament makes manifest."[1]

The concern for communication that has led to linguistic adventures has continued through church history. It is mirrored not only in the struggle to write down what we now call the Bible, but also in deciding which of the ancient manuscripts should be accepted as part of the Bible, and in translating these books from Hebrew and Greek into the languages of today, often over the intense opposition of religious professionals, who knew the potential power of words. The struggle to translate truthfully is still with us. People have recently become aware of the male bias of most translations of the Bible. Almost all Bible translators until recently have been men. They have been dealing with a book out of patriarchal times, but often they have gone out of their way to produce a translation more male biased than the original. Ruth Hoppin in her article "Games Bible Translators Play"[2] has given many examples of this tendency. For example, a word that clearly means "children" in Greek was translated as "sons" in John 1:12 in the King James Version.

Translators also seem to want to harmonize the Bible more than is warranted. A few years ago a nun Sharon met was teaching a high school religion class (all young women). She was trying to help them see that the Bible does have feminine images for God; so she asked her students to find the feminine image for God in Deuteronomy 32:18. None of her students could find it. They were all bright, and the teacher couldn't understand what was wrong. Then she realized that they were all using the Jerusalem translation of the Bible. Here words which are usually translated as "the rock that bore you" and "the God that gave you birth" were changed to "the Rock who begot you" and "the God who fathered you." This "harmonization" is especially deplorable when one looks at the original Hebrew of this passage and discovers that the words translated in masculine terms actually refer to a woman's experience in childbirth—obviously a feminine image.

Those of us not skilled in Hebrew and Greek face a problem at this point. We are reading translations that may be more sexist than the original. A new translation of the Bible that will give careful attention to these concerns will be published soon. Until then, it is a good idea to read a passage from several different translations.

The overriding message of the Bible calls all of us to be equal before God and one another. Individual passages, because of their historical context, may or may not support this thesis. It is appropriate to paraphrase many parts of Scripture to make them more inclusive in language.[3] This is in keeping with the basic concern of sharing the fullness of the Gospel, which the Scripture writers had. It is similar to Clarence Jordan's paraphrases of the Scriptures, in which he placed New Testament events into a new context. When reading a paraphrase in a worship service, we should state that we are reading a paraphrase. Telling the ancient message in inclusive language can help it come through with a new power and personalness.[4]

The primary way in which the faith continues to be communicated is through worship services. Thus the concern for clarity of words that Jesus expressed so forcefully and that was continued in the early church should still be ours today, especially in worship. The words *communion, commune,* and *communicate* have a common root, and one of the most powerful means of communication is the communion service. In it words and action combine to express God's love for us all. If we are concerned about meaningful worship, we must be concerned about language.

SOCIOLOGICAL AND PSYCHOLOGICAL SUPPORT

The field of psycholinguistics is still relatively new, and the study of sexism in language is one of its newest aspects. However, a number of fascinating studies have recently been published.[6]

A lack of clarity and an abundance of outright confusion accompany the use of the male generic. For many years grammarians have held that appropriate English usage calls for masculine nouns and pronouns to stand for all people. Thus we talk about the study of "man," all "mankind," being "sons of God," showing our concern for "brotherhood," and we use the pronoun "he" to follow sexually indefinite pronouns such as "anyone." Common sense alone has caused many people to question such usage. What conclusions can be drawn about men and women if men are always identified with the norm, with human? Are women somehow different?

Even some of the finest writers exhibit confusion in the use of generic language, falling back on male-specific examples; their *thinking* isn't generic. "Man's vital interests are life, food, and access to females" (Erich Fromm); "Man's back aches, he ruptures easily, his women have difficulties in childbirth" (Loren Eiseley). But now sociological studies have been added to show conclusively the effects of such language usage.

In one study college students were presented with a series of statements containing "man" and "he." Rather than responding inclusively by indicating that such terms referred to either or both sexes, the students tended to identify the subject as male. Males were selected 407 times and females only 53 times. The tendency clearly is to image male when generic language is used even when the context would easily allow male and female.[6]

In a second study college students were asked to submit magazine and newspaper pictures as illustrations for a projected sociology textbook. Two types of topic labels were provided for the illustrations: (1) generic labels such as "political man" and "urban man" and (2) sex-inclusive titles such as "political behavior" and "urban life." Those students asked to illustrate "man" titles came up with a significantly higher percentage of pictures that contained males only (64 percent as compared with 50 percent provided by those who were illustrating the sex-inclusive titles). As did the first study, this one showed that a large number of respondents do not picture females as well as males when they come across the terms *man* and *he.*

Linguists themselves are beginning to become aware of this fact, especially since more women have joined their ranks. The National Council of Teachers of English has recently published a book entitled *Sexism and Language.*[9] It contains a provocative discussion of the problems of generic usages and an excellent practical set of guidelines for avoiding this and other sexist usages (parts of this are reproduced in the appendix). One of the writers points out that no less an authority than the *Oxford English Dictionary* now says that the use of *man* as a generic term is obsolete.[10] When prestigious dictionaries begin to admit that the language is changing from its sexist bias, we have hope. The problem of generic usage is only one of many problems in our language today, but it is particularly striking and damaging.

Another related study illustrates the overwhelming significance of language for our lives. The result of this study, originally published in 1973 in *Perspectives in Biology and Medicine* (vol. 16, no. 2), was reprinted in 1978 in *Co-Evolution Quarterly,* with a new preface added by the author, W. C. Ellerbroek, M.D. In it he explained that although the study concerned acne he was primarily interested in why people get cancer. He believes the two maladies are closely connected but that "experts" would be so resistant to his ideas insofar as they concern cancer that he had to relate them to acne in order to get published. It was still seven years before the article appeared in print.

Dr. Ellerbroek developed a special treatment for "hard-core" suffers of acne, people who had tried numerous cures without success. His theory was that these persons developed acne because of a deep-seated feeling of being picked on and that this was caused not only by external events but by the words they used to describe themselves. Ellerbroek reasoned that if these words could be changed these people could break out of their psychological bondage and move toward cure. He therefore worked with them to change their language about themselves and thereby to change the way they perceived themselves. Depending on how certain questionable cases should be counted, at least 80 percent of Ellerbroek's patients showed 80 to 94 percent improvement in eight weeks. No other method of treating chronic acne sufferers that has been scientifically studied obtains these results. In fact, a 50 percent rate of clinical improvement and patient satisfaction would be considered outstanding.

Ellerbroek's study parallels in some dramatic ways the highly unusual treatment for cancer developed by Dr. Carl Simonton and Stephanie Mathews-Simonton.[11] Although their method includes a whole series of treatments related to diet and life-style, one of the most important parts of their treatment is visualization therapy. They encourage the patient to visualize the cancer being defeated and to see themselves well again. Their success rates even among persons who have been declared hopeless by traditional medicine are phenomenal.

What both Dr. Ellerbroek and the Simontons are using is the tremendous power of the mind to image things that can make for wholeness and healing on the one hand or for fragmentation and disease on the other. Their work has strong implications for worship. Language peppered with male-dominated words and images cannot help but have an effect. If our concern is for wholeness and equality, then we must be concerned about the ways we use language.

LANGUAGE ABOUT GOD

In worship, we need to be concerned not only about sexist language in relationship to human beings but also in relation to God. In the book *Children's Letters to God,*[12] a little girl's letter to God says, "Dear God, are boys better than girls? I know you are one, but try to be fair." How can God be unbiased if God is male? Sensitive females have struggled with this question throughout the entire Judaeo-Christian tradition. In some ways it is an unnecessary question, because the femaleness of God has always been reflected in our tradition, although much less than God's maleness. Considering the patriarchal tradition out of which it developed, it is amazing that the Bible contains a number of references to God as female.[13]

The more we study the issue of language, the more important it seems to develop better ways of speaking about God. At first we were primarily concerned about sexist language in reference to other human beings. Sharon was the first to question the almost exclusive masculine language for God. She felt that this set up blocks between her and God that need not be. As we began to search for nonsexist images for God (discovering many in the Bible) and for ways of providing balance if sexual words were used, our own ideas about God literally exploded. Imaging God in new ways, different from "Father, Son, and Holy Spirit" with emphasis on the "Father," brought us entirely new ways of relating to God and understanding God. We had been participating in what is fairly common among most American Christians, an idolization of God through the use of an impoverished vocabulary for talking about God; to limit God to masculine names—and just a few at that is to insist that a *part* of the truth about God is the *whole* truth. We recently completed a film called *The Vision* that tries to express some of this reality.[14]

As we began discussing some of these ideas with others, we found out that many people had strong negative reactions to the traditional concept of God as Father. Because of bad experiences with their own fathers, they could not accept a God cast in the same role. It is true that Jesus said we should call God "Father" (actually a better translation would be "Daddy"), but we have literalized that statement to the point of idolatry. Even Jesus conceived of God in many other ways. By limiting our imaginings to one word, we have done violence to the depth and breadth of God.

We are not suggesting that the word *Father* be eliminated from worship vocabulary. It is an important theological concept that in Jesus' time was utterly new for the devout Jew who was not even willing to name God. Such naming moved us from worshiping an unknown God to one who can be approached as easily as a human parent. But we have two parents, and it is equally important to address God as Mother. In Jesus' patriarchal day, such an address would have been considered ludicrous, but today it is essential if we are to maintain the essential truth Jesus was after, that God is like the best we know in human parents—in their accessibility, their complimentarity as male and female, and in their continuing love for us.

Limited and one-sided imagery for God tends to justify the patriarchal patterns of society. If God is male, then doesn't it stand to reason that all that is best is also male? Identifying God with the male leads to unhealthy psychological responses on the part of both males and females. It tends to reinforce society's emphasis on the male as the authority figure and the female as the submissive one. If the ultimate authority figure is male, should not the rest of the world also be so structured?

Such an understanding of God is also used as a means of excluding women from leadership in the church. Some groups still maintain that since Jesus Christ was male all priests must be male, for they stand in a direct line from Jesus. Jesus of course stands in direct line from God, who of course is also male. Such arguments tend to disintegrate when God is shown not to be male and the maleness of Jesus is shown not to be essential to the meaning of incarnation—God in human form.

Finally, exclusive male imagery for God tends to add a heavy weight against women who wish to become conscious of their equality with men. It is as if the guiding force of the whole universe is against women really becoming equal.

Language about God can be changed to include more sexually balanced images. Some guidelines for doing this are included in the appendix. Such change is crucial for obtaining wholeness in worship.

PRACTICAL CONCERNS IN CHANGING LANGUAGE

The need for working on language change in worship is clear, but it is often a long way from recognizing a need to doing something constructive about it. We wish we could report complete success in this area, but must admit to a sense of frustration. Part of the reason is the constantly changing congregation that attends worship in our campus ministry. We also lack finesse and understanding of how best to bring about change. People have deep-seated prejudices in relation to language, and these are continually reinforced by most of our media and institutions. Those persons who insist that language is a trivial matter and that we should really be concerned about more important issues are often the ones most upset if changes in language are suggested. We think we have had some success in changing people's attitudes about language, and we have certainly learned much from our failures, so we share the theology for change and strategies for change that we have found helpful.

A THEOLOGY FOR CHANGE

Letty Russell's discussion of a resurrection hermeneutic is helpful in developing a theology for change.[15] Dr. Russell reminds us of the story of the two disciples on the road to Emmaus (see Luke 24:13–35). The disciples are trudging along the road toward home, puzzled and discouraged about the crucifixion of Jesus of Nazareth. A stranger joins them and begins to interpret the Scriptures in a new way. Their hearts burn within, and they invite the stranger to have supper with them. As he breaks bread, their eyes are suddenly opened, and they recognize the Christ. Dr. Russell sees this story as a paradigm for all profound change. It shows first that change can occur in community—where two or three are gathered. It happens as the community is led to understand its basic documents of faith, the Scriptures, in a new way by the Christ. Its result is finally a total change in the persons involved; their hearts, minds, and even their language are changed, and they want to share this with others.

God is still present through the Holy Spirit to aid us in this same kind of discovery. The insights of feminist theologians concerning the liberating power of the gospel for women and men are of the same nature as the Emmaus Road experience. Just as that experience changed people totally, so can this one. Only by continuing to be open to Christ's Spirit, can we discover the new ways in which God wants us to change and grow.

STRATEGIES FOR CHANGE

We were among the first to be concerned with changing sexist language in worship. In the early years we were lonely, and we still feel lonely at times, but significant change is taking place. One of the first problems we encountered was in working with other people who shared in various forms of worship leadership in our campus ministry. This was particularly difficult with our midweek communion service, because a different musician was involved almost every week. The problem was in trying to interpret our concern without appearing to be "nay" sayers. It was easy to sound self-righteous and condemnatory, and we sometimes managed to do this fairly well. How could we present the language concern in a way that people could understand and care about when it went against all their teaching in both school and church? This continues to be a perplexing problem.

Early on we decided to distinguish among what we demanded of ourselves, what we asked of others in roles of worship leadership, and what we accepted from our congregation. We found that we could demand from ourselves and could adhere without too many problems to nonsexist language and to sexual balancing. Inclusive language is really clearer language, and with a little practice it can be used unnoticed in free church traditions that are not tied to particular hymns, prayers, and translations of the Bible. We have come to believe, however, that such invisible inclusiveness, although a good place to start, is really selling out the language issue in the long run. At some time each congregation should be challenged to deal consciously with the language issue. Maybe the best time to do this is after several months of invisible inclusiveness. The issue can also be presented in several stages, starting with a concern for inclusive language about people and then moving into language about God. It often helps to introduce new terms for God first as simile rather than metaphor, for example, "O God, who like a mother" rather than "O God, our mother."

We also found that we could ask other leaders to be aware of this concern and, at least in those parts of the service shared by all, to respect it. Nonsexist liturgies have become much easier, with the advent of nonsexist worship resources. We found it extremely difficult to have nonsexist congregational responses when working with our own denominational hymnal or with most contemporary folk songbooks.

We tried to make clear to soloists that inclusive language was a concern of ours and why, but in certain situations each musician was responsible for his or her choice of music. Some sexist lyrics crept in, but we tried to balance this at other points in the service. We also tried to accept the position of our congregation on the matter. They needed as much affirmation as possible for participating at all in a service. We discovered that if individuals in the congregation reacted negatively to every sexist comment at spontaneous times in worship, the result was to stifle comments. Students became afraid of unknowingly "saying something wrong." Now we try to encourage absolute acceptance by both leaders and congregation in this part of the service.

Change on this issue comes gradually, and aggressively forcing it tends to backfire.

When we began to push aggressively, we discovered that what is intended to unite, divides. Some people reacted negatively even to minor changes in spite of the fact that the change had been discussed at length beforehand. In retrospect we see that much of our problem was not because we made changes, but because our reasons for making the changes were not the best. Our book *Women and Worship* had just been published, and we imagined ourselves in the vanguard on this issue. We saw our worship services as models, and we were particularly concerned about being embarrassed if a guest visited our worship services and discovered sexist language being used. Our concern for change was thus in part motivated by self-interest rather than by deep concern for and care about our particular congregation.

Ken Keys has written in *Handbook to Higher Consciousness* that "you add suffering to the world just as much when you take offense as when you give offense."[16] That statement in itself has always given us offense; however, overstated as it is, it contains some truth. Part of our problem in worship for some time was that we were always looking to take offense. We delighted in going to services just to see what was wrong with them! For that matter, we still find some delight in this perverse occupation. For some time now though we have been struggling to discover a way to work for change not out of a spirit of offense, which tends to breed hatred and anger, but out of a spirit of abiding love and care for the particular persons with whom we minister. At times we are embarrassed by the sexist language and theology that creep into our services, but we are closer to making a real impact on the consciousness of some people with whom we work.

WE ARE NOT ALONE

One of the rewarding aspects of working on this issue for a number of years is seeing real change take place. The battle is far from won, but some encouraging signs are now visible. We have already noted some of the sociological and psychological data that support a concern for language change and show the importance of language in our lives. The work of the National Council of Teachers of English in their *Sexism and Language* and of various book publishers is also heartening. Almost every denomination now has task forces working on sexist concerns in religion, and part of their work is dealing with sexist language in the church. Commissions on worship of various denominations have also been struggling over this issue. The United Methodist Commission on Worship, for instance, recently made a policy decision that no publications put out by the Commission on Worship would use sexist references for people and that every attempt would be made to see that references to God were sexually balanced. The new Lutheran Book of Worship (ALC/LCA) has attempted to eliminate sexist references for people in many of its hymns, and Roman Catholic publishers of contemporary church music, such as Pastoral Arts Associates and North American Liturgy Resources, have also taken steps to eliminate sexist references for people.

It is important in working for change in a local setting to call upon all the resources you can. It is helpful to encourage persons in your congregation to read studies such as those we have sighted, to study books such as this one and *The Liberating Word,* and to examine nonsexist worship resources such as *Sisters and Brothers, Sing!* and *Because We Are One People.*

Although this chapter has concentrated on the spoken word, recent studies show the importance of nonverbal communication. Gestures, eye contact, posture, clothing, tone of voice, and facial expressions all communicate. Communication is most powerful when the verbal and the nonverbal reinforce each other. When they are in conflict, communication loses its integrity and seems ineffectual. If we are concerned about communicating a gospel of wholeness (salvation,) we must strive to use both inclusive language and nonverbal cues that express wholeness and love. Such simple gestures as hands outstretched as if to hug the world can speak powerfully of the universal power of God's love. On the other hand, constricted gestures, or the lack of gestures, can speak volumes about an unhappy life—this in spite of a message of Christian joy. Ideally, our verbal and nonverbal language should be in harmony. When they are not, we may find our words outshouted by the rest of our body.

4

All God's Children

ONE OF the favorite songs of our worshiping community is "All God's Children" by Ruth Duck. The first song in our hymnal *Sisters and Brothers, Sing!,* it reflects the essence of wholeness in worship. It reminds us that *all* God's children are precious to God, regardless of their age, race, sex, or handicap. In this chapter we will discuss some of those who are often left out of worship services and what can be done to include them.

WE ALL BEGIN AS CHILDREN

We tend to forget that we all were children once. We especially seem to forget what it felt like to be a child. Perhaps that is why the little person is frequently ignored in worship.

David Holmes in his booklet *Involving the Little Person in Worship, Part II*[1] suggests some questions to ask oneself that help re-create the feeling of what it is like to be a child in a worship service. For example, how would you feel if everyone in front of you stood up and you could not see over them? How would you feel if someone began speaking to you using a vocabulary in which every fourth word was unknown to you? How would you feel if no one who looked or thought or acted like you ever had any kind of leadership position in worship? It is much easier to describe the problem than to do something about it. How do we include children in worship without bringing the whole service to a kindergarten level?

PART TOGETHER, PART APART MODEL

Many congregations who have struggled with the need to include children in worship have used a model in which part of the Sunday morning service is for families and part is for older youth and adults. Although this fractures each service, it has some unique advantages. It takes seriously the different emotional and intellectual needs of adults and children. It recognizes that, whereas valid and meaningful worship can happen for people of all ages together, this automatically precludes discussion of perplexing intellectual concerns of the faith. Rather than attempting to sneak these in occasionally and hope the children will be quiet during them, these areas are reserved for the adult part of the service. On the other hand, singing, dancing, simple drama, beautiful films, and provocative stories can be shared with the entire congregation.

The most usual pattern is for everyone to begin worship together, and then after the first third or half of the service the children go to other rooms for activities relating to the same theme as the adults are considering. Sometimes the children come back for the last bit of worship together. We attended a church in which this was done in two stages. For the first fifteen minutes or so, people of all ages met together for spirited singing and movement. Then the preschool children left for separate classes. More singing and a drama based on the Scripture lesson of the morning followed. After this, children through third or fourth grade left for their classes. The third section of the service consisted of the sermon and responses and times of community intercession in prayers and sharings. Families were reunited after the formal service.

Another possibility is to begin the service apart and come together for the last half or third. Sometimes everyone can meet together for the whole service; other times for the first part and still others for the last part.

THE CHILDREN'S SERMON

One of the best-selling books at any ministers' conference is a book of children's sermons. Mainline Protestant pastors especially seem to be blessed (or cursed, depending on how you look at it) with being expected to give a children's sermon in each worship service. And almost every pastor who does so has been told by some adults that they get more out of the children's messages than they do out of the "real" sermon. Such a statement can be ego deflating, especially if the minister has spent weeks on the "real" sermon and only five minutes on the children's sermon. It may be, however, that these comments are an expression of the need all of us have for simple, concrete, clear story sermons. Perhaps the regular sermons should be turned into messages that children can enjoy and understand.

Children's sermons as they are generally presented in Protestant services have a number of problems. First, they tend to say to children that the rest of the service really isn't for them. They have three minutes, and the adults have fifty-seven. Three minutes is of course better than none. Second, the pastor is often tempted to use the children during the children's sermon to entertain the adults. This can damage the child's sense of importance and portray the church as being basically dishonest.

The children's sermon, however, may be the best option in particular situations, especially when a congregation is in the initial stages of involving children in worship. When it is not manipulative or devoid of imagination, it can help children feel important. In some churches the children's sermon is presented in the early part of the service, and immediately following it, they leave the service for activities elsewhere.

CHILDREN'S LITURGIES OR FAMILY LITURGIES

Another option, used especially by Roman Catholics, is the children's or family liturgy. These liturgies are subject to misuse just as children's sermons are. They are sometimes seen as an occasion to impress adults with the cuteness of the kids, or as an alternative to grappling with the difficult problem of worshiping intergenerationally. In these cases, such liturgies take over the old-style fundamentalist concept of the "children's church." On the other hand, at their best, children's liturgies (sometimes called family liturgies—for the whole family of God), are some of the most exciting worship experiences in our churches today. They can show even the most doubting skeptic that it is possible to do intergenerational worship that is meaningful to everyone.

SOME MYTHS ABOUT WORSHIP WITH CHILDREN

In designing services for children and adults it is important to recognize some myths that have been part of our thinking. The first is that children cannot understand the deep mysteries of faith. The obvious question is, Who can? Children are steeped in fantasy and symbol and may come closer to appreciating mysteries such as the annunciation, the resurrection, and the ascension than adults. Our older child is currently "turned on" to superheroes, who provide our modern equivalent of fairy tales; he is open to the unexplainable.

Watching our young son in play is a real delight. Usually we don't have to be with him long before we see him using fantasy. In five minutes he can be Wonder Woman, Batman, Spiderman, and Cinderella, in that order. As he plays with toys in his bath, he sees them first as what they are—then suddenly a bubble-bath bottle becomes a boat, a bird, or a person. Children, especially the very young ones, are probably those in our congregation most able to celebrate the mysteries of faith in all their delightful wonder.

A second myth concerning children is that they have short attention spans. Certainly, children cannot generally sit through boring speeches for twenty minutes at a time. Adults might be better off if they protested such an experience too. The notion, however, that a child's span of attention is as long in minutes as the child is old in years is simply not true. Even very young children will spend hours watching TV. They can certainly be expected to be fairly intently interested in some particular part of a worship experience for at least five minutes, maybe more. It is good, however, to pace worship that involves children more quickly and with more variety than is found in most "regular" worship services.

BACK TO THE BASICS

How do we develop liturgy that holds a child's attention? It is important to get back to basics. The simple, strong symbols of the faith and of our everyday lives are usually the most effective tools. A unifying symbol for each family liturgy is often helpful. Our faith is full of them—water, fire, butterflies, flowers, air, dirt. A child is familiar with these things, but now in worship he or she is helped to discover them in new ways that help them understand something of the mystery of life.[2]

A child who enjoys the beauty of a butterfly in flight can be shown how that butterfly emerged from a dead looking chrysalis and how similar its emergence is to the resurrection. After the child has learned that the butterfly has long been a symbol for resurrection within Christianity, he or she will be reminded by each sighting of a butterfly of a basic Christian concept.

Storytelling is an effective means of communicating with children (or anyone for that matter). Jesus used it often in his ministry. The part of the sermon people almost always seem to love is its illustrations (the stories). Long after we forget everything else about a sermon, we remember a story or two, helping us recall some truth in it. Instead of regretting that only the stories are remembered, we should affirm this fact and plan sermons accordingly. Not only would this involve the children more, but everyone else would be more interested too.

A good source of stories with profound ethical truth is children's books. Children's authors may be some of the most profound prophets in our society today. Through their sensitive, yet simple stories, they often show us more clearly how God wants us to live than do the most learned theologians. One of the best ways to get acquainted with these books is to go to your local children's library and spend some afternoons reading.[3] Children's films are another good source of story material.

SOME OTHER THINGS NOT TO FORGET IN PLANNING WORSHIP THAT INVOLVES CHILDREN

Finally, remember that children usually need more physical activity than adults. They need opportunities to move around, and dance and other kinds of simple activities can provide these opportunities.

If worship occurs in the usual church with pews, families with small children can be encouraged to sit near the front so that the children can see what's happening. Music is a great joy for most children.[4] Hymns for a family liturgy need to be accessible to children in both vocabulary and rhythm. The same is true with any of the other arts used in worship. Often, however, we underestimate what may fascinate a child. Modern dance or a Gregorian chant may be more deeply moving to a child than twenty choruses of "Jesus Wants Me for a Sunbeam." The key is to plan a variety of experiences in worship, many of which will appeal in special ways to children.

Children, especially younger ones, need to use the large muscles of the body. Sometimes they demonstrate this need in a traditional service by getting loose from their parents and running up and down the aisle. It is possible, however, to make time for using these large muscles in the worship service. One of the most natural times is the offering. Children and also adults often find great meaning in participating in an offertory processional in which everyone gets up, marches to a designated spot, and presents their offerings. Dances and processionals to hymns or special music also provide opportunities for total body movement. Children might also be asked to come forward at some time in the service to do or see something special for them.

Since we minister in a campus setting, children are not present in most of our worship services. We have come to consider this a loss. We need children. We need their honesty and spontaneity. We even need their anger when events don't go as they wish. Jesus said that we must approach God's reign as a little child. It is much more difficult to do this if children are banished to nurseries or in other ways excluded. "We're all God's children, and we want to be whole." This wholeness can best be enabled when we are together at least part of the time.

INCLUDING OTHER AGES IN WORSHIP

What we have said about children also applies to people of other ages. Although youth are often highly valued in local churches, the people planning worship services still largely ignore them. They may ask for an occasional youth participant, but he or she is usually asked to do something on adult terms in an adult way. This may account for their wanting to shock adults when youth are "turned loose," usually once a year to "do their thing." They are determined to "let it all hang out" the one time they get. Would there not be ways to involve youth regularly in the planning of worship? How about finding out what religious songs they really like? What movies are important to them? Would any of these songs or movies be appropriate for worship, either as is or in a sermon developed from them? Do the youth of your church have particular talents that could be shared regularly in church? A youth choir is grand, but is that the only option? What about drama? multimedia? dance? other forms of music? What are the religious questions the youth of your church are asking? Could some of these be the basis for a series of services?

Old people are also often ignored in worship. Unless they are the only ones still coming to a church, they are seldom asked to fill leadership roles. Their particular talents are often forgotten. If the church is attempting new kinds of worship to involve people physically, older people are often forgotten. If the congregation is going to dance together, consider those who may not be able to dance, either physically or emotionally. They should be provided options that are not embarrassing. Old people are often the "living history books" of a particular place. They can enrich the whole community of faith.

INCLUDING BOTH SEXES

In the chapter on inclusive language the importance of including both male and female in worship services was emphasized, but the issue goes much deeper than words alone. Unfortunately, most worship services are still almost totally male dominated. It is no accident that lifeboat drills call for women and children to go first. In many ways they have similar status. Women often feel left out in the same ways that children feel left out.

The most obvious way in which women are often left out of worship is in leadership roles. Until recently, many denominations have not allowed women to be ordained. The number of ordained women is increasing, however, and most congregations are more open to women assuming leadership roles in worship services. The ideal in worship leadership is a balance between male and female, old and young, and so on. For example, if the pastor is male, he can be balanced in leadership by a woman. There is no reason why only one other person need be chosen to assist at each service. Several people can have meaningful leadership roles in worship so that persons of both sexes and of different ages can participate.

Sometimes when a congregation decides to involve more female leaders in worship, they discover that many women in the church do not want to be leaders. This is not unusual, since this may be the first time they have ever been asked to assume such a position. Often their reluctance is due to a lack of self-confidence. We have found that participation is more likely (especially in a large church) if some basic training in worship leadership is offered. This is also an excellent opportunity for some adult education in the area of worship.

Women are also left out of worship services in subtle ways. Perhaps in the pastor's sermon illustrations men play the significant roles of responsibility. Perhaps the pastor never bothers to preach on any of the great women of the Bible. Perhaps the pastor makes condescending comments or rude jokes about women. Perhaps women never hold any of the significant power positions in the church.

At another level, any service that is usually weighted toward the masculine side of the chart in Chapter 1 leaves out women, because it undervalues and underuses those aspects of worship with which women have most characteristically been identified. The service is poorer for everyone, because the richness of what women have traditionally offered both in worship and to society as a whole is missing.

INCLUDING ALL RACES, CULTURES, AND RELIGIONS

Black, Hispanic, Asian, and Indian peoples have long known and practiced wholeness in worship.

In a black gospel service today the congregation takes an active part in the total sermon, lifting up the leaders and helping them to sing and preach with greater enthusiasm and eloquence. They move their bodies rhythmically and sometimes dance. Healings and experiences of great emotional release are not uncommon. These people have a story to tell, and they come together to share this story in new, yet old, ways each week.[5]

The same is true of Hispanic worship. Roberto Escamilla has described Hispanic worship at its best as "Fiesta Worship."[6] In it worship is a celebration of God's victory in Jesus Christ, a rejoicing in the gift of life. Worship is focused on a fiesta (a feast)—communion. The joy of dancing to a Mariachi band is joined with the tenderness and love of the *abrazo* (the embrace). The hurts and pains of the world are taken seriously, but the congregation refuses to be defeated by them, and the predominant mood is joyful.

Similar experiences occur in the worship of Asian and Indian people. Each group has a richness to bring to worship. If we ignore these contributions, we are the poorer for it.

It is not always easy to know how to incorporate contributions from other ethnic groups into a setting that may be predominantly or totally white, mainstream American. It is inaccurate to assume that white people just wouldn't be interested in "foreign" styles of worship. An example of interest in ethnic customs is the rather rapid change in eating habits in the United States. Twenty years ago almost no ethnic restaurants could be found in any but the largest metropolitan areas. Most grocery stores stocked little but good old "American" food. Then ethnic groups migrated to less populated areas and opened restaurants, and food chains began to make ethnic items available in grocery stores. Today it is hard to find someone who has not tried Chinese food or eaten a taco, and more and more people are beginning to celebrate the richness found in foods typical of other countries. This kind of mixing can also occur in worship, which is, after all, a kind of banquet. A nice change from the usual opening hymn that begins worship would be a Dakota Indian hymn, complete with drums and dancing. This would guarantee the congregation's attention from then on in that service. We have found that a congregation is usually a bit more willing to try something daringly unusual if it is from a different culture. For example, an African benediction that involves embracing has often been readily accepted because it comes from a different culture and tradition.

We know a church whose congregation includes recent immigrants from the Scandinavian countries and people from England, Germany, and India. Even those persons of somewhat similar backgrounds have markedly different traditions of worship. One of the most exciting community-building experiences in that church has been the opportunity for people to share their heritage with one another. This has been particularly possible around Christmas.

One way to help people become interested in other worshiping traditions is to visit the service of another cultural group. Some of our students visited a black church and came back anxious to start singing some of the beautiful songs they had heard.

What we have been saying about other cultures and races is also true about other religions. If we have a basic faith foundation in Christianity, we can claim some of the richness in other traditions. We have much to learn from traditional Indian religions about oneness with the land and respect for nature. We have already gained much from Eastern religions concerning the meaning and practice of meditation. If in our studies of other religions, we discover something of beauty—a poem, some scripture, a liturgical act—it is appropriate to share this within the context of a Christian service. This needs to be accompanied, however, with information about the religion and an explanation of why it is appropriate for a particular service. All religions have major differences, and these differences should not be minimized. All religions also have much in common, and at times it is appropriate to celebrate this commonality.

A FINAL CONCERN

At times it is a frustrating dilemma to attempt to be inclusive of many different realities at once. Something borrowed from an ethnic group may be sexist in language. A song that is beautifully inclusive of women may be musically poor. It is important to strive for balance. It may sometimes be necessary to settle for something less good musically to get the kind of words you really need for a service. Working toward wholeness in worship is a long-term project. If the teaching and example are consistent, a congregation will increasingly demand the best.

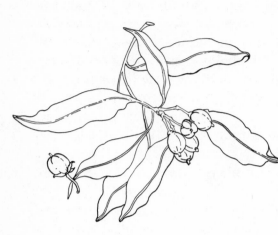

5

Concern for Healing: The Pastoral Focus of Wholeness in Worship

JESUS SAID that the well do not need a physician. He came to the needy, those who are sick. In an increasingly "healthy" society, such words might cause concern until we realize that in some way or other all of us need the physician. People who are handicapped in obvious ways—the crippled, the blind, the deaf —have been helping us realize this truth anew. We are all handicapped, but some of us are handicapped in more immediately obvious ways. Who is to say, however, that a person twisted by an inability to love is less handicapped than someone crippled by polio? Who can say that someone blinded by jealousy is less handicapped than someone who has been physically blind from birth?

The more we have been exposed to this understanding of the handicapped, the more we feel that it is exactly what we need to understand the pastoral focus of wholeness in worship. Worship can only be whole when it is meaningful to people with any kind of handicap.

Although it is easy to see what to do about making a church accessible to people with obvious physical handicaps, it is usually difficult to do anything about it. "Why should we make our sanctuary accessible to people who can't walk? Nobody in our congregation is crippled?" The reason for there being no crippled congregants may well be that the sanctuary is inaccessible to people who can't walk. Such people have already been effectively driven away. Steps may also present a problem for older persons. A fall or other injury may keep them away for months until they can once again climb steps. Costs for making churches more accessible to persons who cannot use steps may not be prohibitive. Hydraulic chairs on an open stairway are a possibility if the number of persons needing the service is not great.

Professionals who work with the blind, with the deaf, and with those who have learning disabilities can be helpful in analyzing church facilities. An ecumenical approach to this problem may be a way in which to avoid duplication and make more services available. For example, the churches of a city could work together to provide one good place for those with learning disabilities to come for worship, education, and recreation, rather than offering such a program at all the churches. The same might be true about a deaf ministry. On the other hand, it is important for us all that the physically handicapped participate at least some of the time in an ordinary worshiping community of faith. To encourage this, at least some services should be planned with opportunities for persons with particular handicaps to take part.

It is more difficult to identify the less obvious handicaps, but no less important to minister to them in worship. Worship services, as they are usually structured, contain a model for moving toward wholeness. We come to worship as hungry, needy people, willing in some way or other to bow before the presence that is greater than we are. We rejoice in that presence through song and other acts of praise. We also are called to be honest in this presence through confession. Through Words of Assurance or Prayers of Pardon we are helped to know that we

are loved in spite of the ways we have failed. In the freshness
of that knowledge we are prepared to hear with power the word
of God's love for our life today. Finally we are physically fed
(communion) and sent back into our everyday lives with the
command to share what we have heard and experienced. People
who talk about the way worship renews (even refuels) their
lives have been open to this *healing* model that is repeated over
and over again.

Much can be done within this model to minister to the heart
handicaps of our congregation—the loneliness, hatred, jealousy, lack of self-worth, and so on. Congregations, however,
need the option of even more focused services dealing with
inner and outer healing. For the past year or so we have been
experimenting with healing services in our campus ministry.
Such services are conducted after our regular Wednesday evening communion service. Sometimes no one attends. At other
times ten or twelve persons have been present. In the service we
have provided an opportunity for specific prayers for particular
persons. These prayers have often included the laying on of
hands. We have not witnessed spectacular healings, but we
have seen enough to be convinced of the validity of this service.
Persons are invited to request prayers for both physical and
emotional healings, and although many have sought inner spiritual healing, most have concentrated on physical healing.

This whole area is frought with dangers. People's expecta-
tions may be raised in unwise and invalid ways. Lack of obvious healing may make some question their faith. Healing
services are often associated with a naïve theology, and irre-
sponsible leaders tend to take advantage of people already
weakened by illness and pain. This does not, however, negate
the possibility of conducting responsible, meaningful, and effective healing services. To forget this area simply because of
its difficulties is to give up an effective way of dealing with
handicapped people.[1]

An effective tool for helping people begin to deal with their
inner hurts is fantasy. The early church used fantasy Bible

study a great deal to help people become familiar with the Scriptures and begin to have life-changing experiences.[2] Some examples of this are given in chapter 12. As we (particularly Sharon) have done these fantasies, we have seen people moved to the point of tears. Deep places inside them are opened up, and they begin to work on problem areas.

Another gateway to the inner life is dreams. We must be at least as open to hearing about dreams in worship services as we are to hearing the latest scholarly interpretation of Scripture. We can still remember with a sense of great excitement the first worship service we attended in which someone related a dream along with part of what she felt God was trying to tell her through that dream. Sounds just like the Bible, doesn't it?

6

Concern for the Whole World: The Mission Imperative of Wholeness in Worship

AT ONE time mission and worship were inseparable. The early Christian community used many words interchangeably to refer both to the church's liturgical and to its social activity, for example, *diakonia, koinonia, leitourgia,* and *eulogia*.[1] Worship and mission were linked by the early church because they were inseparable in Christ's own ministry. Christ taught that it was counterfeit to worship without being involved in acts of reconciliation (see Matt. 5:23, ff.). If mission is understood as all that works toward furthering God's love in the world, and if worship is seen as a celebration and affirmation of this love, then Jesus' life and ministry are the living demonstration of mission and worship combined. The proof of this unity is not found in isolated biblical texts, although these are numerous, but in Christ's triumphant reign over all the world. Not only did Jesus die for the whole world, but he was raised that all might come to know God's love. The whole world is God's worship house.[2]

No wonder the apostle Paul could say with such enthusiasm that we are to present our *bodies* as a *living sacrifice,* which is our spiritual *worship* (see Rom. 12:1). We worship not just in pretty sanctuaries, but everywhere. All ground is hallowed by the God of all creation.

Unfortunately the news of the sacredness of all the world does not penetrate most of us most of the time, and so we need special times and places to affirm this truth. We need opportunities to share with others the glimpses of God's love that we have received in tangible and intangible ways. We need times of separation from the world so that God's love can be enfleshed again and again.

The unity between mission and worship has often gone unrecognized. It is not at all uncommon today for social activists and evangelists to consider worship a luxury they can't afford; and liturgists seem not to want to be bothered by the corruptness of politics or the imperative of evangelism. Both groups need each other desperately. Without worship, social action and evangelism when successful become prideful; and if they are not successful, they become sullen and cynical. Worship without concern for mission quickly becomes isolationist and unreal.

A World War II story illustrates how worship without mission can become isolationist. A cultured couple in Germany hosted an elegant dinner party during the height of the war. They had the finest tastes and provided the best food and drink for their guests. They exhibited great sensitivity and love for each other, real care for their guests, and beautiful appreciation of great art. They were splendid hosts, but the party occurred within sight of the smoke from the gas ovens of a concentration camp. Somehow all the finest entertainment and the most cultured caring for a particular small group was soured by the stench of burning bodies.

Worshiping congregations cannot carry on polite charades of pleasant community sharing in the midst of a world that still has far too many gas ovens. Worship that is not always sensitive to this ghastly part of the world is unfaithful and heretical. Worship that is whole is infused with mission.

Even times of praise and thanksgiving are mission related. Why do we praise? Because God is the universal ruler of creation who can help us bring all things to goodness. The Old Testament leaders understood this. They helped people to see that all the old idols—sun, moon, stars—could become part of the chorus of praise of the one true God. What would happen if we began to see modern idols in the same way? Can atomic power, television, even the lowly surfboard contribute to a paeon of praise to God? The goal of mission can be seen as the increase of thanksgiving (see 2 Cor. 4:15, RSV). The more we help people direct their lives into an attitude of thankfulness, the more we have helped increase the love of God in the world.

The church's times of prayer in worship are not only preparation for mission. If we believe at all in the efficacy of prayer as a world-changing activity, then the church is just as much in mission when it is in prayer as it is when it is on a picket line. In Ephesians 6:18 prayer is referred to in the context of the weapons of warfare against the alien powers that threaten love in the world. Authentic prayer, however, almost always impels us to action. Prayer is dangerous to someone who doesn't want to get involved. It inevitably pushes us into the particular ways we are called to make a witness for love in the world.

It is out of such times of searching prayer that protest masses and pray-ins often come. Such visible combinations of worship and social concern may sometimes be only a clever public relations gimmick, but at their best they are deep expressions of the unity of mission and worship.

Some of the most moving spiritual experiences of our lives have happened when we dared to throw ourselves into the heart of profound social and political conflict. Tom's sharing with black brothers and sisters in marches and pray-ins was his baptism into the depth of Christ's call to involvement. Sharon's involvement with women's rights has led her to new insights about power and community.

A few years ago several of us from the Wesley Foundation joined a number of Christian groups in a Holy Week protest concerning human rights violations by governments around the world and the involvement of our own government in permitting and sometimes even encouraging this activity. We formed a human tabloid of torture on the steps of the Capitol and others places in Washington, D.C. As we shared with other concerned Christians in this dramatic act, the power of Paul's command to present our bodies as a living sacrifice to God, "which is our spiritual worship," invaded us. Our bodies were on the line, and we felt, however imperfectly, some of the sufferings of our tortured sisters and brothers around the world.

The mission power of worship is highlighted in prayers of intercession. In our own congregation we have a period of joys and concerns each Sunday. This has become a time of intense tenderness and power as people share, sometimes to the point of tears, a burden or a concern. We pray over each of these concerns as a gathered community in the firm conviction that our prayers make a difference. Sometimes a concern is shared again a few weeks later as a joy, when the situation has changed for the better. We are not claiming magical powers for prayer. We are not saying that a gathered community's prayers can always bring exactly what we think we want, but such prayers can help to bring healing and new understanding, no matter what the outcome of the particular crisis, and we have seen these prayers transform the outcome.

Mission is obviously involved in other parts of the service such as the Scripture readings and the sermon. Scripture is at its heart an account of God's love for the world and God's command for us to be agents of this love. Faithful sermons can hardly be anything else.

The time of confession, if this is a regular part of a service, can also be mission directed. Confession should remind us of the reality of evil in us and around us. There are many ways this can be accomplished: from the reading of newspaper headlines showing our inhumanity to one another to the praying together of a classic prayer of confession. Our recognition of the power of evil in the world heightens our awareness of mission concerns by reminding us of our need for the church's mission and by keeping us from being too prideful in our task—evil is indeed *in* us as well as around us. We are not driven to despair by this admission, however, because confession is followed by the Words of Assurance or the Prayer of Pardon. These keep us focused on God's love, which will not be defeated by evil, no matter how ferocious that evil may seem.

The offering is obviously a time to focus on mission. In our congregation we have tried to emphasize this as a time to be concerned with more than just money, a time of real rededication of our whole beings. We still believe this, but perhaps we have deemphasized money more than we should. J. G. Davies has shown that for Paul the collection of money was no small matter.[3] Paul twice referred to the monetary collection as the *koinonia,* which is usually translated "fellowship" or "community" (see 2 Cor. 9:13; Rom. 15:26). Paul was seeing this money as a metaphor for what the Christian community could be and do. He knew that it could be a powerful force of love and caring. In 2 Corinthians 8 and 9, Paul not only called the contributions *Koinonia,* but also *charis,* or grace. Have we been too timid in asking for money? Could we not see the offering as an opportunity for the gathered community to energize their grace? Perhaps part of our timidity has come from our failure to use the offering for real mission. Perhaps the offering and its use needs to be reevaluated in terms of Paul's poetic insight.

Communion is of course a parable of mission. It makes visible Christ's concern for sharing. It recognizes the physical needs we all have and how these are interwoven with spiritual needs. It reminds us of the awesome power of evil, which could break Christ on the cross, and of the even more magnificent power of God in the resurrection. It sends us forth fed, but with the gnawing truth in our bellies that none of us is fully fed until we all are.

Any blessing after communion is anticlimactic, but it can still serve to reinforce what we have just experienced. It can be a sending forth of the congregation to be God's love in a hungry world.

Whether we look at individual sections of worship services

or at the central meaning of wholeness in worship, we are con-
fronted by the significance of mission. Worship can never be
whole if it is insulated and isolated, serving just a few select
groups. God's love knows no limits, and our care as shared in
worship must reflect this vastness.

7

The Arts in Worship

THROUGH the arts we find a primary way of probing the mystery of God and of all creation and of experiencing that mystery emotionally. When the arts are ignored or considered unimportant, worship becomes a head-oriented desert of intellectualism.

Many of the values crucial to wholeness in worship are found in the arts, for they deal most often with the concrete and the particular. They probe the depth dimension of life, which cannot be fully expressed in words. They trigger our emotions in response to the truth toward which they are struggling. They understand that reality is not a neat package to be wrapped in philosophical propositions but a vast canvas that needs to be explored over and over again.

This chapter will focus on the arts and worship. We will look in some detail at several art forms—dance, drama, film, music, and visual arts—and suggest some specific ways in which these forms might be used creatively to bring about wholeness in worship.

Any generalization about "the arts" can only be partly true. A drama and a piano concerto are different in obvious and significant ways. Thus what we say about "the arts" applies to most specific art forms, but it is always more true for some than for others. The function of art in worship or in life can never be fully explained, and this is part of the power of great art.

Dmitri Mitropoulos was once asked to explain the extraordinary effect his conducting had on both orchestra and audience. He wisely answered that he wouldn't even try to explain for fear he might become like the centipede who was asked by a humble little bug which of his hundred legs moved first when he walked. Bursting with pride, the centipede began to analyze the question and has not walked since.[1] Any discussion of the arts must necessarily be incomplete, but it can be helpful to try to discover some basic understandings of the arts and worship.

The Swiss painter Paul Klee said that "art does not reproduce the visible; rather, it makes visible." The Russian writer Leo Tolstoy said that "the function of art is to make that understood which in the form of an argument would be incomprehensible." We "understand" things in many different ways and at many different levels. Tolstoy was speaking about a knowledge that is in part beyond ordinary words. As a dancer said when asked to explain her dance, "If I could explain it, I wouldn't have to dance it."

Most of us have had moments when we were overwhelmed by a work of art. It has penetrated to the heart of our being, but a verbal expression of the experience is not possible.

A major function of art for our lives, and hence also for worship, is to bring order and clarity out of the muddiness of everyday life. By ordering reality with brush, pen, or body, the artist brings to us a new understanding of what life is about, an understanding that is much more focused and planned than the chaos of ordinary living.

In worship this ordering function of art is beautifully expressed in many services through the prelude. Here the musician as artist takes the ordinary chaos of sound and orders it into harmony, rhythm, and movement. Like all art, it is a reenactment of the creation in which God formed beauty from the chaos. It is a symbolic reminder of this creation and therefore a musical call to worship.

To order and clarify reality does not mean that great art is therefore unambiguous. Because it deals with a reality that is finally not fully expressible, it is never absolutely clear itself, but it is clearer than our ordinary lives and therefore it can address us with tremendous power. The author Thomas Mann wrote that if the German writers had, through their fiction, made richer promises than Hitler, it would have been Hitler, rather than the writers, who would have had to flee the country.[2] Through art all our dreams, fantasies, prayers, and promises can be expressed. One place where the power of the arts can come together is in worship.

The arts in worship (again as in life) usually leave their mark in two different ways. The artist serves as priest and prophet. As priest, the artist brings beauty, helping us to see in fresh, breathtaking ways. Great art can sometimes "take our breath away." It is truly inspiring and therefore is the vehicle of the Holy Spirit, who gives breath and produces inspiration. Part of what we do in worship is celebrate beauty, in God and in the creation. Art helps us breathe in this beauty and make it a part of ourselves.

For several years we have used the five minute film *They Shall See*[3] in a variety of worship settings. It is a poetic expression of the beautitude "Blessed are the pure in heart, for they shall see God." The filmmaker has taken an exquisite combination of nature scenes in regular, slow, and accelerated motion; regular, macro, and micro shots; and combined them with a beautiful soundtrack of instrumental music. The effect is overwhelming. It has always produced in the persons viewing it a sense of reverence and awe. Perhaps the same thing might be accomplished by a talented naturalist if she or he were to lead a group on a four-hour hike, but this is done in a five-minute film that transforms an ordinary sanctuary into a panorama of God's beauty.

The artist also functions as prophet, the bringer of truth (sometimes unpleasant) about ourselves and our society. The Canadian educator Marshall McLuhan has called great art a "DEW line, a Distant Early Warning system."[4] At its most significant, art can show us our weaknesses and point toward what will happen unless we change our ways. Thus artists are what critic Bernard Scott called "spiritual alarm clocks"; they shake us up and bring us to focus. They keep us honest through irony and satire. They keep us sensitive through poetry and story.

The artist as prophet shines forth most prominently in worship through our times of confession and proclamation. A few years ago we planned a Good Friday service in which we encouraged the congregation to reflect on the crucifixions we participate in today. This was enabled by several short dramatic sketches, from contemporary poetry and drama, which showed specifically and powerfully our inhumanity to each other. This service did not please everyone, but it did touch those in attendance.

Particular art forms can inspire worship, but worship itself is also an art form. The liturgy planner resembles the theater director. She or he puts together a dramatic extravaganza. The drama has a clear rhythm and movement (often from praise to confession to proclamation to dedication). The artistry of the director comes in putting together all the varied pieces of an ordinary service to make it an extraordinary event. He or she is responsible for the set (the appearance of the sanctuary), the script (the written part of the liturgy), the music, dance, and any other art forms used. The final production should include audience participation; the congregation is among the actors in this drama. Whether or not this production is inspiring depends on the skill and artistry of the worship director or directors. Persons who would hardly dream of trying to produce even a simple one-act play without a director think nothing of throwing together a worship experience with little thought for its possible artistic unity and power.

Some cautions are important in thinking through worship and the arts. The first involves the "artist" in worship. Some who call themselves artists attempt by that label to force a snobbery upon a congregation, imposing their own particular tastes on everyone. Some church musicians and graphic artists insist that only a particular kind of music or a particular style of art is appropriate in the church. They often insist on doing things in worship "for the good of" the congregation. More and more professional artists are coming to recognize that art is not wrapped up in a particular type of music or painting but that it is instead part of a truthful expression about life, which can come in any form, whether it be a grand piano or a comic strip. The form appropriate to a particular worshiping congregation will depend on that group of people. This doesn't mean that one should never attempt to educate a congregation into an appreciation of a different style of art, but it does mean that this education should most often be in the context of creative artistic expressions in forms the congregation already appreciates.

A second caution is that subject matter is not necessarily a clue as to what art is appropriate in worship. If art is to be judged on the basis of how well it makes visible the truth about life, how much it inspires us with its beauty and truth, then we must admit that literally tons of ineffectual, inauthentic "works of art" which, while having a religious subject matter, say nothing to us as human beings. Such "art" is not art at all. It is instead a cheap kind of illustration. This is especially a problem in "religious" drama. It is far better to use a "secular" piece that speaks truthfully than a "sacred" one that is false at its heart.

A third caution is that it is generally best to emphasize those art forms that can actively involve the congregation as a whole. If liturgy is truly "the work of the people," then the people should be involved as much as possible in the artistic expressions of worship. Thus, it is usually better to use hymns than arias, group dances than solo dances. Of course, sometimes the mood needed in a particular service can best be expressed by a soloist. When possible, however, it is good to strive toward total active involvement.

Part of the essence of art is to do the best one can. In one sense, therefore, the ultimate art is living, and artful worship can help to enable the art of living. In worship we are called to bring our very best to God. In giving our best, we receive new power and strength from God. This is what artful worship is all about, and it is the essence of wholeness in worship.

DANCING

For some time, disco dancing has been the big craze. It's hard to know what will come next, but almost certainly some kind of dance will always be popular. We are physical beings, and need to express the music inside us. What better way than dance?

Dance can be defined as any rhythmic movement; therefore, one doesn't have to be a professional to dance. Any human being can move with some rhythm.

Dance and music have many parallels artistically. It is interesting, therefore, that music is central to most worship services but that dance is often banned or ignored. Many churches employ a full-time music director, but we have yet to hear of any church that has hired a full-time dance director.

Part of the problem is that dance is physical. We can't dance without using our bodies, and many in the church have a deep fear of the body. We can sing with just our vocal chords, although any good voice teacher will tell us that we really can't and that the more we use our body, the better we sing. In singing, however, the body can recede into the background; in dance this is impossible.

The need to reintroduce dance[5] into worship is thus thwarted by some of our ideas about the body and sex. We need to proceed with care and sensitivity in this area, not only because it can enhance the beauty and integrity of worship, but also because it can help liberate us from some of our negative feelings about the body.

Dance can be gradually, yet firmly, introduced into the life of a worshiping community in several ways. Outstanding solo dancers and small dance groups (perhaps from a nearby college or university) can be invited to your church on an occasional basis to dance the Scripture, a hymn, or an act of praise. If your congregation is conservative, these first dances need to be simple and directly related to obvious religious material. More abstract expressions can come later. The dancers' costumes should be modest. Dancers in tight leotards are not generally the best introduction to sacred dance.

At the same time this kind of special dance is being introduced, try to involve the congregation as a whole in some simple rhythmic movements. Sometimes even learning deaf sign language to a hymn or prayer can be a beautiful, nonthreatening introduction to congregational dance. Simple elaborations of the passing of the peace, a short musical response to prayer, and a gesture in preparation for prayer are other possibilities,[6] as are congregational processions during a hymn or the offering, and in churches where it is not common, kneeling for at least some of the prayers. For ten centuries church members did a simple dance movement to many of their hymns. Called the tripudium, it worked with any song in 2/2, 3/4, or 4/4 time. It consisted of three steps forward, one step back, three steps forward, one back. In a sense the dancers were proclaiming a theology with their feet. They were affirming Christ's victory over an evil that is still obstinately present, a victory that moves the church forward but not without setbacks.

When we were asked to plan a worship service at Garrett-Evangelical Theological Seminary, we decided to incorporate the tripudium in it. Traditionally, people in the congregation linked arms, often several abreast, as they moved around the large open spaces of the great cathedrals. Most churches in our country, including the Garrett-Evangelical chapel, have narrow aisles. The best we could do was line people up three abreast and get them moving. The result was a bit chaotic, but also glorious. For the first time in memory, faculty, students, and guests danced together in worship. Students especially thought it a grand experience in equality.

DRAMA

Drama is much less threatening to most congregations than is dance. Most persons can see that worship already has a dramatic character. The drama developed from a holy play, the purpose of which was to assure the cycle of life. It was performed at decisive moments, seedtime and harvest, midwinter and midsummer, and has been incorporated into the worship life of all the great religions.

Drama has been so well accepted within worship because people have sensed that our relationship with God is basically dramatic—one of question and answer, movement and counter-movement, the interplay of creation and re-creation. In drama we are asked to put on, to personify, someone else. To find others in yourself is not only the secret of drama but also of forgiveness and love. God, the one who breathes life into us, at the same takes our life into himself/herself and bears our guilt. The Christ event is thus pure drama.[7]

Perhaps because drama is immediately more acceptable, a great many resources have been developed for its use in the church. Unfortunately, almost all these resources are, at best, second rate. They are like much "religious" art—illustrations of some theme or moral rather than deep grapplings with basic truths about life. Therefore, in our worship services we use primarily secular drama, adaptations of parables and stories, and impromptu drama.

SECULAR DRAMA

Many of the truly religious plays are not listed in drama catalogs under "religious" but are works for the secular theater, both past and present. Most are far too long and involved for an ordinary Sunday service; however, many contain particularly appropriate scenes that are full of dramatic power as well as grace and truth. They often work well in particular worship settings as part of the sermon or as a call to confession. They must be introduced carefully and played with sensitivity and skill. We have found that particularly the works of Tennessee Williams and Arthur Miller have great possibilities for worship.

ADAPTATIONS OF PARABLES OR STORIES

For a number of years we have cosponsored, with other campus ministries at our university, a drama group that tours churches in our part of the state with a short play suitable for use in a regular Sunday morning worship service. By far the most successful of these plays have been those adapted from other genre, usually the short story. Different groups have toured with dramatic adaptations of *Hope for the Flowers* by Trina Paulus, *The Velveteen Rabbit* by Margery Williams,[8] and *George and Other Parables* by Patricia Ryan. One group also had good success putting together a number of contemporary Christian poems in a dramatic reading entitled "Christ among the Television Trees."[9] This doesn't mean that no good short religious plays suitable for congregational worship exist, but it does mean we have had difficulty finding them. In some ways, adapting another medium may bring the actors closer to the creative import of what they are doing than simply acting a set script.

IMPROMPTU DRAMA

This is perhaps the most satisfying method of using drama in congregational worship that we have found. It can include everything from brief little vignettes the two of us do as part of a sermon to an entire dialogue drama to various sorts of interruptions during the service.

Impromptu drama, as we use the term, does not necessarily mean without rehearsal, although that is a possibility. It usually means unscripted for the most part, although it may be rehearsed a great deal. In addition to various types of dramatic sermons such as first-person monologues, historical dialogues, humorous skits, and "devil's advocate" dialogues, we have also had some exciting times involving the congregation. If the technique is not used too often, a planted interruptor in the midst of the sermon has great dramatic effect. Sometimes our services are interrupted by a visitor playing the role of an Old Testament prophet or a contemporary questioner. It has also been exciting to work with small groups in developing a dramatic presentation for worship around a particular theme that is largely or completely original.

Another method we have tried is splitting into groups in a worship service and asking each group to develop a short dramatic skit that expresses the truth of a particular Scripture or theme. This has generally proved disappointing. Most people are uncomfortable and embarrassed in such a situation. At best they try to play for the laughs of the others. Part of the problem, however, is that an ordinary Sunday worship service lasts only about an hour. If groups had more time to work together, the results might be more creative.

Like all the arts, drama at its best can touch our deep emotions and our unconscious. We are therefore called to use it as effectively as we can in worship.

FILM

Isn't film just electronic drama? Sometimes it has been conceived as such, but it is an art form all its own. Perhaps because it has been available only for the past few decades, it is still largely unused by most congregations.

Because we live in the "age of television," we have become a visually aware people. The technical quality of what we see for hours a day on television is generally outstanding. If we are to use film or videotape in worship, we need to be aware of what most of our people are already accustomed to.

Although we see quantities of technically good visual material every day, this doesn't mean that we necessarily really "see" it. We may experience it mostly with half attention, distracted by a hundred other things around the house. In worship we can focus our attention more and therefore "see" in new ways. Also we can see material that is often not shown on commercial television. Its technical quality may not always be as good, but its artistic and social concern aspects can make up for this.

Some people object to the regular use of film in worship. They claim that an effective film tends to overpower everything else. A quality film used appropriately can be very powerful, but something powerful can be powerfully good.

Nevertheless, we must be especially sensitive to the power of film. Several years ago Tom showed the film *The Eighth Day* as part of a call to confession in a worship service. He had not prepared the congregation for the impact of this film, which contains some excruciating scenes of atomic destruction. Several people were brought to tears, and one person was so sickened by what she saw that she had to leave the service. Upon evaluation Tom felt largely to blame. Tears are not necessarily bad in worship, but the people should have been prepared for what they were to see. Using the film early in the service was also probably poor planning; it was so powerful that the rest of what was done lost its impact. That kind of film would probably be more effective at the climax of a service. It seems as natural to us to have at least one short film or multimedia production (slides, music) in each service as it is to have an anthem each time. In some ways our culture is more in tune with receiving visual experiences than they are with receiving aural ones. Films can come almost anywhere in the service—as an act of praise, a call to confession, a Scripture interpretation, part of the sermon, a call to commitment. As with anthems, timing and suitability are important. Short films, five minutes or less, are the most flexible and therefore the most useful in most worship services.

Many persons have been defeated by technical problems in trying to use film and other media in worship. One problem that often seems insurmountable is darkening the worship area. Screens are now available that do not need much darkness, and a rear projection box screen can be used even in regular light. Many technical problems arise in using media in worship areas, but we have not as yet seen one that could not be at least partially solved with ingenuity, hard work, and some money.

Commercial films. The number of films produced each year is astounding. As with books, it is almost impossible to keep up with all that are released. Also, as with books, if you keep searching long enough, you will almost always discover a film dealing with just the topic you want. The quality of the film is another matter.

We have found that films produced specifically for the religious market are often inferior. Recently their technical quality has been improving, but they are often artistically insensitive and much too concerned with preaching a message. A good religious film, however, will fit most naturally into a worship service.

Many so-called secular films also work beautifully in worship. It is usually necessary to relate the film to the service through comments or discussion either before or after the film. Some of the films, both religious and nonreligious, that we have found most useable are listed. A brief description is included along with at least one source where the film can be obtained.

Sources for obtaining films should be carefully checked. In most areas excellent free film service is available through the public library system. Most denominations have excellent film libraries for their conference, region, or diocese. Even if your denomination does not have such a library, you may be able to join that of another denomination. Films obtained through such a system are much less costly than those of commercial outlets. Many universities also have outstanding film libraries and rent their films considerably below the cost of commercial companies. Check out what's available in your area first, but many universities, such as those in Illinois, Indiana, and Michigan rent their films nationwide.

Your own films. With the advent of inexpensive super 8 equipment, home videotape units, and Polaroid instant movies, it has become possible for a local congregation to make their own films and other media products for worship. This takes much time and some money, but it is usually worth it.

A few years ago Sharon was given responsibility for a confirmation class of junior-high students in a large older church. As part of their learning together she asked each of them to make a short film. She loaned them inexpensive super 8 cameras after giving them a quick lesson in how to operate them. After the films were shot and developed, she helped the students to edit them into one twenty-minute film. She had it soundstriped and helped the students add their own soundtrack. On confirmation Sunday, this film became most of the sermon. It was a moving and exciting experience, especially since some students had shot film at the church and people in the congregation got to see themselves on the screen.

Such media experiences take lots of time, some expertise, and some money, but so does a good music program. We have nothing against music, but it seems strange that most churches will assume a substantial commitment to it without even considering a commitment to multimedia. Some churches might be able to use a media director more effectively than a music director. Most young people we know are more interested in making a film than in joining a handbell choir. The costs in equipment and time are about the same.

Again, like music, film can be misused. It should never be employed just to fill up time. It should not be used if it cannot be done right technically. Used with sensitivity and care, however, it can be a powerful way of reaching a congregation.

MUSIC

All that we have said about music thus far might lead you to believe that we have some prejudice against it. On the contrary, we recognize the immense significance and importance of music in worship. We simply wish that some of the other art forms could be equally as well utilized. Music has been called the language of the gods. People long ago felt that it had great magical properties. As late as 1316 the Council of Cologne forbade the singing of the famous hymn of mourning *Media in vita in morte sumus* for anyone unless special permission were given. The song of death, it was believed, could actually bring about death.[10] Still today scientists are investigating the healing properties of music, and music therapy is a growing field.

The power of music has not been ignored by advertising. Madison Avenue knows that one way to sell a product is to sing about it. They know that music has a way of getting inside us and then coming forth to remind us of an idea or a product.

Almost anyone who has grown up in a worshiping community can attest to the power of music in their lives. Certain hymns and other songs of the faith have gotten inside us and helped shape us.

Because music is powerful, we need to question the way it

is used in many worship services today. For example, is it appropriate to use music merely as "filler," so that the minister can walk from communion table to pulpit? Even musical parts of the service that earlier had great theological significance have been reduced to filler status. Most people assume that the purpose of the prelude is to provide something for people to listen to while latecomers are still arriving. If everybody were on time, we would quickly go on to something more important. The prelude, however, is the formal opening of the worship service when the musician takes the randomness of chaotic sound and orders it into something beautiful. It is thus a reenactment of creation and calls us to remember the way in which God formed the universe out of chaos.

Another question concerns the choir. What is its purpose? Is it to help lead the congregation in singing or to perform for the congregation? We have nothing against the concept of performance in worship *per se*. We understand this to mean giving music your special, personal form.[11] We feel, however, that most choirs have become too performance oriented and have almost entirely forgotten their function of leading the congregation in singing. Not only are choirs too performance oriented, they often perform music that is inappropriate for the intended audience (the congregation). Most church choirs only sing classical compositions from other centuries. People in the congregation who are not classical music lovers, are expected week after week to listen politely to music that is not what they would have chosen. If part of the purpose of worship is to speak to the gathered community, then care should be used to find the vocabulary (musical style) that can do this best. In most cases, we suspect it would not be classical music. Other musical styles —whether plainsong, folk, jazz, country, or pop music—have much to contribute to worship. And, of course, the music selected should be of as good a quality as possible.

The same thing is true of the music the congregation is asked to sing. It is almost all from other centuries in a style foreign to their daily lives. The popularity of folk and jazz masses is due in part to their use of a musical language that is more familiar to most people. We are certainly not pleading for the elimination of all the great old hymns of the church, but we are asking for a balancing of these with some of the great new songs of the church.

We developed *Sisters and Brothers, Sing!* not only because of our concern for worship resources with inclusive language but also because we felt a need to share with the church at large some of the excellent new music being written. Each church needs not only a "regular" denominational hymnal with all the great old hymns, but also at least one and maybe several newer hymnals or songbooks that contain contemporary music. Ideally, churches could develop their own loose-leaf collections of hymns both old and new.

A few summers ago Tom was helping lead a workshop in Nashville with the editor of a leading denominational hymnal. In a discussion of music for the church, the editor held up two copies of the hymnal and said he felt it was a pretty good book, one that every church ought to have a couple copies of. The problem, he claimed, is they have hundreds of copies and that is *all* they have. Here was someone pleading for less use of the book he had edited, emphasizing instead the need for variety and imagination in the use of music in worship. It is not good to be tied to any one hymnal no matter how excellent it may be. We need to venture forth with new songs, both those that are explicitly religious and those that are secular but speak powerful truth.[12]

THE VISUAL ARTS

When 16th-century reformers destroyed religious art, it was not because they felt it was silly but because they feared its power. They were afraid that ignorant people would mistake the object for what it represented and therefore be guilty of idolatry. Now we welcome art of certain kinds into our church buildings, but we use it for decorative purposes. Congregations that build new churches often distribute a pamphlet to explain the symbolism for their members and friends. If these symbols had arisen out of the life of the congregation, a pamphlet would be unnecessary. The pamphlet simply shows that most of the symbolism is obscure or antiquarian and thus communicates nothing to the congregation upon whom it has been imposed.[13]

Good liturgical art makes us aware of that which is beyond ourselves. It points to the presence of God and thereby keeps us from the most common of idolatries, the worship of ourselves. Bad liturgical art, on the other hand, serves to clutter up the place. It points to nothing except shoddy work and thinking.

As with all the arts, including the visual arts, the need is to facilitate and encourage good visual artists while at the same time opposing cheap decoration. Unfortunately, especially with visual art, cheap decoration is often actually "cheap" in cost and more what people have become accustomed to in thinking of religious art. We need to view visual art with a keen sensitivity to beauty; we should not become absolutist about particular pieces. Solomon's *Head of Christ* is probably not good art by most critical standards, but in many churches it has been a part of the hearts and lives of the congregation. To them it has become beautiful and acquired meaning far beyond what the artist originally intended. We must be sensitive to such feelings as we work to bring better visual art into the church. We must often be satisfied with compromise in this area, believing that as people are gradually introduced to a great art lesser art will lose its appeal.

The chief function of church architecture is to provide a stage for common worship. It needs to be physically adequate, that is, have proper heat, light, and acoustics, and be emotionally satisfying. It should feel like a place of worship. Finally and most important, it must function in a liturgically effective manner. The design and placement of the liturgical centers—pulpit, altar table, baptismal font or baptistry—should reflect the theology of the worshiping congregation. This means that the congregation should be consulted when a church is built or remodeled. Most really fine architects prefer to work this way. They want to know the congregation's concept of what the church is and what it does when it worships. Since almost all architects work on much the same fee arrangement, search until you find one who is sensitive to your congregation and willing to work with them in designing or redesigning a building.[14]

Most people who see a church building never enter its doors. By its visibility a church building is a witness for or against our faith. Hardin, Quillian, and White[15] point out that the building answers the following questions. (In many ways almost all visual art does the same.) (1) *Is it relevant?* If a church clothes itself in a period costume, it is saying "no." (2) *Is it sincere?* When a church uses cheap materials that pretend to be something they are not, and pretensions as absurd as the false-front stores used in the movies, it says "no." On the other hand, spending millions in an attempt to go "first class" calls into question the sincerity of the church, which calls for identification with and concern for the poor. (3) *Is it presenting a faith that is significant and meaningful?* If its architecture is a silly hodge-podge of other periods or of modern offices, schools, or fads, it is saying "no." Visual arts are for all to see. We must take care that what people see is an expression of the gospel we claim to believe.

Another way in which the visual arts have prominence in worship is through the garb worn by worship leaders, who have been encouraged in recent years to use increasing varieties of clothing. The old black robe of many mainline Protestant ministers has been replaced by white, and in many instances it has become an alb, chasuble, or poncho. The designing and making of these garments is an excellent project for a group or particular gifted individuals in a congregation. A whole set of garments, of different styles for different seasons of the Christian year, is a significant contribution to more beautiful worship. The Christian year can also be the inspiration for many other art projects: slides, banners, paraments, and posters can add richness and meaning to a worship area.

8

The Senses in Worship

THE ARTS are sensual, and we have touched upon using the senses (especially sight and hearing) in our discussion of worship and the arts. It seems necessary, however, to think specifically and in more depth about involving the senses in worship.[1] The senses are a primary path to knowledge, and to ignore them in worship is to forget one of the most significant ways in which we learn. Since we have elsewhere discussed sight, hearing, and touch, we will concentrate in this chapter on smell and taste.

SMELL

Our society has been made extremely sensitive to smell, at the same time we have been taught to mask many natural odors. Sales of deodorant, mouthwash, and air fresheners generate millions of dollars each year while heightening our awareness of the reality of smell; yet in many worship services we act as if this sense did not exist.

Incense has a long and noble tradition in Christian worship. It is still much used in Eastern Orthodox and Roman Catholic services. If persons from outside these traditions are uncomfortable with the swinging incensors, they ought not rule out incense all together. Incense can be burned in many less ostentatious ways and thereby help to create a mood.

The effect of smell on our beings has not been totally explored,[2] but it is known that smell and memory are somehow connected. Smell can trigger a particular memory of long ago or a feeling of anxiety or joy that is linked to an occasion when that aroma was present. Special scents in worship may remind us of worship at other times in our lives. Some real estate agents claim that a house that is shown when the smell of fresh bread baking is prominent inevitably seems to sell better than a house without this captivating odor. Whether that smell is universally associated with good times and good food or whether it is just inherently pleasing, it seems to be a real motivating force. Isn't it too bad that we serve bread so often in church without that wonderful odor? We need to experiment with ways of allowing the smell of fresh baked bread to permeate our sanctuaries on a Sunday morning. "Do this *in remembrance of me.*"

Another interesting experiment with odors in worship can be done with a scent game that can be purchased at toy stores. Each game has about ten or twenty fairly realistic scratch and sniff scents. These can be incorporated into a discovery prayer, with each person sharing something about that scent as a prayer to God. All the scents do not necessarily have to be pleasant. Many prayers of confession or intercession could be triggered by the odors of our increasingly polluted world. Consider the Old Testament concept of a God who is offended by the stench of injustice in the world (see Amos 4–6).

It is also good to remind worshipers of the scents that are already a part of worship—burning candles, bread and wine, one another.

TASTE

When receiving communion we experience the sense of taste; it is therefore important to use good quality bread and wine (or grape juice or both). The type of bread and the kind of wine or juice can vary with the mood or theme of the service.

For example, in a service focusing on our need for penitence, a hard Russian rye bread and a slightly bitter wine or grape juice laced with a tiny bit of vinegar could be used. In a service focusing on the joy of God's love, a sweet, soft bread and a sweet wine or juice might be used.

Taste may be used in many other ways in a worship service. In some churches a sweet bread is shared during the love feast at the close of a service. Coffee, tea, or juice with donuts may serve the same purpose. Some of Jesus' teachings rely on our sense of taste. For example, in a service centered on his statement that we are the salt of the earth, the actual taste of salt could be meaningful. In one such service each family was asked to bring a salt shaker from home. During the sermon each person tasted salt from the shaker. Together the congregation reflected on what it means to be the salt of the earth. They were then admonished to remember that they were the salt of the earth each time they used the family salt shaker.

Other foods can also be meaningful in worship. For example, a liberation meal could include milk and honey, reminders of the Exodus and the struggle of the Hebrew people to reach the promised land—the land of milk and honey. The honey can be served in the milk or on crackers or in a milk wine; it could also be the liquid center of honey candy. Paul wrote about the need for Christians to move away from milk to solid foods. In a service based on this passage, cheese could symbolize the solid food of the faith to which we are called.

OTHER OBSERVATIONS ON THE SENSES

We have mentioned the importance of human touch and contact; the sense of touch is also important in other ways. Several years ago we attended a service in which the theme was growth and creation. The worship leader had brought in huge buckets of dirt. As part of our worship we were to experience that dirt with our hands, our nose, in any way we wanted. We also planted some seeds in it.

Another innovative way of experiencing the senses of sight

and hearing is to create a visual and auditory electronic environment. Instead of being something that we focus our attention on at some definite part of the service, this environment functions like banners and paraments and stained glass windows— there for us to appreciate all during the service. This environment, however, is changeable and can be moving. It can be created by a combination of slides, continuous films, overhead projectors, tape recorders, and lights. A great deal of work and some skill are involved, but the effect is worth it. Many people feel we are so overstimulated by electronic media in our ordinary lives that we need simplicity in worship, not another show. We tend to sympathize with this point of view, but a tremendously moving worship experience can be stimulated by an electronic environment.

Using the senses in worship requires common sense and an understanding of what will be appreciated by a particular congregation. All of us, however, can find more effective ways to celebrate the senses in worship.

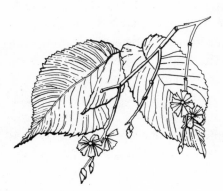

9

Valuing All Our Times—Past, Present, Future; Good, Blah, Bad

A priest was asked: "How many people were at the early celebration of the Eucharist last Wednesday morning?" He replied: "There were three old ladies, the janitor, several thousand archangels, a large number of seraphim, and several million of the triumphant saints of God."[1]

IN WORSHIP we are connected with the saints of the present and with the "whole company of heaven." It is therefore transgenerational; in it we remember and affirm not only all different ages of people present today but also all the ages of history. In worship we are together in Spirit not only with people all over the world but with a family of Christ that has rejoiced and grieved in the catacombs and feasted in the palaces of kings, as prayers and hymns of other times remind us.

A knowledge and an awareness of tradition bring a perspective on the height and depth of our faith and helps us to sense a oneness and wholeness with the Christian family down through time and in the eternity of heaven. The basis of wholistic worship is tradition. Tradition is valued not as the Pharisees perceived it, as the protector of vested interests, but as the midwife to new birth.

Geddes MacGregor has pointed out that a green shoot does not grow out of midair; it grows out of a healthy old tree. It never looks better than when it grows from an old tree that has been tended and loved for generations. Some new shoots may take odd shapes; but as long as the tree is properly pruned, new growth will adjust in time.[2] The vision of worship that we describe in this book is not created from nothing; instead it flows from a rich tradition.

Although our worship is rooted in the past, it flowers in the present. It is important to affirm and celebrate past traditions, but it is disastrous to be bound by them. A perennial temptation is to idolize the past at the expense of the present and the future; but we need to see the bad as well as the good in tradition. We can celebrate the healings of Jesus' day, but if healings don't occur today, something is wrong. We can marvel at how Jesus fed the thousands, but if people are not being fed because of the gospel today, something is wrong. Worship must be firmly planted in the present.

Many people in mainline churches are so interested in remembering the past history of the church that they forget they are a part of continuing history. Unless we are open to the Spirit moving in our midst today, we cannot expect wholeness in worship. As Paul said, "*Now* is the acceptable time; behold, now is the day of salvation" (2 Cor. 6:2, RSV).

Although rooted in the past and flowering in the present, we must also be "on tip-toe," as Paul said (see Rom. 8:10, PHILLIPS), in anticipation of the future. Whatever problems we face—ill health, poverty, a bad job, low self-esteem—are finally transformed in the power of Christian hope. We worship in the knowledge that no matter what happens God's love continues through us. God may not make everything just like we want it, but in worship we affirm that the final chapter has already been written and that life is after all a comedy not a tragedy. Without this faith affirmation, worship cannot take on the bright joy that makes it a preview of heaven.

Wholeness in worship comes about as we not only affirm all our times historically but take seriously our present moods and feelings. We are creatures who have good, blah, and bad times. In worship we have often tried to speak creatively about our good times through prayers and songs of praise and thanksgiving. With prayers of confession, words of assurance or prayers of pardon, and prayers of intercession we have recognized our bad times. We have often, however, ignored the blah times, those periods when nothing wonderful or disastrous is happening.

Perhaps the old concept of the liturgy being "the work of the people" is an appropriate metaphor. We usually go to work whether we want to or not, because work is essential to our livelihood. How else to get the money for food, shelter, and clothes? Work has acquired a bad connotation because what often parades as work is really voluntary industrial servitude. Walter Bagehot has said that "the real essence of work is concentrated energy."[3] When worship is viewed by the congregation as their work, a great burden is lifted from liturgy leaders. They no longer have to be entertainers, professional inspirers; instead they do their best to lead everyone in good liturgy work. Unfortunately, in most places today, congregations suffer from a horrifying rate of liturgical unemployment. They think that a few professionals should do everything for them. Often the professionals (the ones who do the work) get much meaning out of worship, but they are the only ones.

We work even when we feel blah because we know the consequences of not working. But what are the consequences of not worshiping? One reason for the ravenous hunger of many for spiritual food, which has led them into cults, drugs, and other religions, is the current state of liturgical unemployment in worship. Without being helped to worship in a personal way, many people turn to other sources to satisfy their hunger. They must be helped to see Christian worship as active participation that demands both discipline and individual freedom, as does all great work. Through the discipline of worship they can be helped to see the validity of keeping on in the spiritual life, even during dry periods. In the individual freedom of worship they can be challenged to do their spiritual work in the way that uniquely fits them.

When we have asked former students what worship services they found most meaningful, they almost always refer to one or several in which they had been intensely involved. Such work was the road to real meaning and significance, a way to value all our times, no matter how we may be feeling.

Liturgy has also been referred to as play. At first blush, this concept would seem to be in direct opposition to the idea of liturgy as work. Creative and happy play, however, is also work as we have defined it—"concentrated energy." When our son first went to Montessori school, we were surprised that his teachers referred to his activities there as his "work." They were simply seeing these playlike experiences as the proper vocation for a three-year-old. Liturgy can be either work or play as long as it is that to which we are called even in our "blah" times and as that which calls forth our concentrated energy.

10
Affirming Word and Table

THE communion service is the primary example of wholeness in worship. The symbols of wholeness are the one loaf and the one cup, which represent the one body and blood of Jesus Christ. The forces of fragmentation are real and vicious. The loaf is broken, the cup spilled, but in the midst of what looks like tragedy, wholeness reemerges. Christ is put back together again in our bodies, in our blood. The one body becomes en-fleshed again in the one spirit that pervades the church as we share communion (the *eucharist,* the great thanksgiving or joy feast) together.

As we share in this simple service week by week, we see it touch the lives of students as nothing else can. Without words, the Word is expressed in all its poetic power and mystery.

Many Protestant churches, however, have backed off from communion. They have relegated to unimportance the most powerful expression of God's loving wholeness for us and omit the very part of Christian worship that makes it distinctly Christian in deed as well as word.

Both of us grew up in Protestant churches that downplayed the importance of communion. At most, communion was cele-brated five times a year. Attendance was usually down on these Sundays. Everyone, including the ministers, saw the service as rather unnecessary, to be enacted occasionally for its historical value. During Tom's first year in seminary, in a conversation with the dean of his school, Perkins School of Theology, he pointed out that he was interested in worship but that communion had never meant much to him and he felt it was celebrated too often in seminary chapel. The dean, Joseph Quillian, was appropriately upset and managed to say something like, "If communion doesn't mean anything to you, how can you possibly be interested in worship? You've just downplayed the essence of Christian worship!"

It was a number of years before these words made full sense to Tom. It has just been in writing this book that he has realized how crucial the service of the table is to worship.

Many denominations may not look favorably on communion every Sunday because they have not celebrated it in imaginative and meaningful ways. Like every other good thing, it can be stultified and routinized until drained of meaning. The pure physical logistics of communion within large churches becomes something of a problem. How do you serve all these people in a reasonable amount of time?

Sometimes the physical problems of preparing and serving communion have been thought through too carefully. Who invented those cardboard wafers as a substitute for the bread? They are certainly cheap, long lasting, and convenient, but they are a poor representation for a Christian central symbol. Their plastic, imitation taste, however, may not be too bad a symbol of what the church and worship has often become.

And what about the wine? Who invented those handy individual cups that so effectively separate us from one another? Although they did not come into general use in Protestant worship until about World War I, by the time of World War II they were more deeply entrenched in some churches than if they had been specifically prescribed in the Didache. This has led Geddes MacGregor to observe that "the newer the tradition the more steadfastly people resist changing it."[1] Perhaps these cups are more sanitary than a common one,[2] although that may depend on how well the individual ones are cared for; but again their use abolishes a central Christian symbol. These little jiggers seem to be saying that Christ's blood was spilled out in carefully measured doses for each follower.

The controversy continues over whether communion should be observed with wine or with grape juice. Certainly wine symbolizes more of the power and vitality that communion is meant to portray, yet the use of grape juice can be a valid protest against the evil that mishandled alcohol can bring. We should be sensitive to all persons on this issue. Some alcoholics have been excluded from taking communion because their church used only wine. Churches that use wine should also have grape juice available for those who cannot drink wine.

Communion can be celebrated in an infinite variety of ways,[3] and if the method is changed frequently, no one way gets too set for the congregation and becomes idolized as *the* way. Communion can also be a more relaxed service than is traditional. Taking communion in some churches is reminiscent of a military drill; everything is ordered down to the last detail. People are told exactly when to come forward to receive the elements, exactly how long to stay, and exactly how they are to return to their seats. All spontaneity is ushered (literally) out of the service. On the other hand, in some large churches people are invited to come to any of several stations around the church. They come whenever they want to wherever they want. Everything is a kind of glorious chaos that works amazingly well and takes no longer than the fully regimented service.

Receiving communion in the pews is sometimes useful. People can see one another as priests if this concept is emphasized in the service, but people remain stationary, and if we want to move people spiritually, we need to move them physically. For this reason, we do not recommend communion in the pews as a usual practice.

No symbol better expresses the tension between fragmentation and wholistic love than communion. It is just as important as the word preached.

Traditionally in "the word" part of the service the Scripture is read and the sermon preached. In this segment of worship the primary record of our faith (the Scriptures) as interpreted for our lives today (the sermon) is presented. Too often, however, worship leaders have taken a narrow view of the way in which the word can be expressed. It does not always have to be read by a single person and exposited through a monologue but can be presented in a myriad of ways—film, drama, dance, mime, dialogues and trialogues, to name but a few. The simple reading of Scripture and sharing of a sermon will no doubt continue to be the usual means of conveying "the word" in most worship services; however, we do encourage you to imagine other ways in which God's Word can be expressed.

The lectionary, in its careful charting of our scriptural history through an Old Testament, Gospel, and Epistle lesson for each week of the church year, is helpful in emphasizing the Word. By basing preaching and worship on a three-year lectionary, for example, a congregation hears most of the essential passages of the Bible in three years of its public worship. The three-year lectionary is now widely used in many different Protestant churches and in Roman Catholic churches, a practice that bridges denominationalism and unifies the church at large. Individual preachers who follow the lectionary will cover all the basic aspects of the Christian faith in a church year.

Many recent seminary graduates are committed to using the lectionary as they develop their worship schedules for the year. Both of us have preached from the lectionary for extended periods; however, it is not the only system that helps one move toward wholeness in worship. At times lectionary preaching can be a convenient way to avoid the real and pressing needs of the congregation and of the world. Lectionary lessons often address contemporary concerns with profound insight and power, but they sometimes do not deal with the issue or the concern that really needs to be addressed that week.

Using the lectionary is one of the best ways to ensure the inclusion of the totality of the gospel message, but we must be flexible in using it. We may need to deviate from it at times. We may even need to try other methods for extended periods, such as preaching on a book of the Bible or on particular themes. No method is perfect or even best for everybody.

11

A Wholistic Approach to Special Services

IN THIS chapter we will discuss four special services of the church—baptism, weddings, healings, and funerals—and ways in which the concept of wholeness in worship can influence them.

BAPTISM

Baptism is the initiation rite of the church, the sacrament that introduces God's unique care for each of us as manifested in the community of the church. Since baptism is not usually a separate service but is performed within a "regular" worship service, it is important to give it the significance it deserves.

Like communion, baptism is a dramatic act and in worship needs to be enhanced rather than diminished. The main physical element in baptism is water, a biblical symbol for new life. It is important that sufficient water be used so that the power of the symbol can be experienced. Too often ministers act as if there were a terrible water shortage. They feel that only a couple of sprinkles of the messy stuff are sufficient. What a way to undercut the power of the baptismal experience.

Each of the three main methods of baptism have some scriptural justification. Immersion, which symbolizes death and resurrection (see Rom. 6:3–4), was most clearly used in the New Testament. It is a vivid illustration of the new birth in Christ and is especially appropriate for adults. Pouring reminds us of the way God's love is poured out upon us at all times (see Joel 2:29; Acts 2:17). Whether we are ready or not, willing or not, caring or not, God still loves us. This mode of baptism is especially appropriate for infants. It seems to say that we are celebrating and affirming the power of God's love to wash over a child through its parents and the congregation, long before the child can even say the word *God*. The third mode of baptism, sprinkling, has some scriptural justification in the Old Testament concept of washing away our sins (see Ezek. 36:25–26). We believe it is by far the weakest of the three methods usually used for baptism. But sprinkling is the most convenient, and therefore it is used a great deal. It is certainly better than no symbolism at all and, especially when used with some degree of liberality, can convey real meaning.

Since baptism is the rite of initiation into the church, some congregations place the baptismal font in the back of the sanctuary. Persons to be baptized and their friends and sponsors gather at the door of the sanctuary and knock, seeking entrance to the household faith. They are received, and then the baptisms are performed at the back of the church; the congregation may turn and face the font or even gather around it. The knocking and seeking entrance can be used even if the font is kept at the front of the church and the main part of the ritual occurs there.

When baptizing infants we often invite the congregation, especially if it is small, to contribute symbolic gifts to the child's "hope chest." These are not to be opened by the child until he or she is confirmed and can include such things as a picture, a poem, a thought, or a favorite Bible passage. The congregation thus actively participates in the service and the child can later relive part of what happened.

We have also used a symbolic baptismal garment that is put

on the one baptized immediately after the sacrament is administered. Often embroidered with an appropriate Christian symbol, this garment can be another visual sign of the child putting on Christ in a new way.

When baptising infants, we use the method of pouring and have sometimes used the tub that the child usually takes her or his bath in to catch the water, especially if it is not too large. We pour the water with a large sea shell, a beautiful expression of God's handiwork in nature. We like to make sure the congregation hears the water splashing and sometimes, as part of the preparation for baptism, have used a film that shows the beautiful wonder of water in various scenes of nature.

Anyone concerned about wholeness in worship has problems with the traditional trinitarian formula that is used almost universally. To baptize someone in the name of the "Father, Son, and Holy Spirit" seems unduly biased toward the concept of a male God. Instead we use "Creator, Redeemer, Sustainer." We have been told, however, these two formulas are not really parallel. One is a series of names for God that encompass a number of particular activities; the other is a series of descriptions for God that may seem to limit God to that particular attribute. One acquaintance of ours believes that she can solve this formula problem by baptizing in the name of the Triune God, one in three, three in one. This preserves much of the historical dimension of the Trinity without getting into particular descriptions or using sexist language. Still others feel that it is important to use the historical formula at this point, balancing these references for God at other significant places in the same service.

Baptism offers a great opportunity for a pastor to do prebaptismal counseling with the persons involved and to share some of the basic concepts of the faith with persons who are about to experience one of the great sacraments of the church. Not to do this is to fall short of the call to wholistic concern that we believe each pastor has.

WEDDINGS

Almost no service of the church offers as much potential for wholeness as a wedding while at the same time containing so much that might prevent wholeness.[1]

Each couple should have the opportunity to help design their wedding service. It is, after all, their wedding, and it should be as meaningful as possible to them and their relatives and friends. We have found that couples often come to remarkable new insights about themselves as they work with a trained pastor to plan the service, which should reflect their values and faith. It should be an expression of what is really important to them and of what they believe about marriage. Therefore we simply do not marry persons without adequate time to counsel with them about marriage and to help them plan the service.

Many traditions that have become associated with weddings are antithetical to wholeness. Whoever said that the bride and groom can't see each other on the day of the ceremony until the service begins? Whoever said that the bride's father must escort her down the aisle? This is, of course, a throwback to the time when the bride was literally bought and sold. It is hardly an expression of the kind of equality that is at the heart of wholeness. Perhaps today it would be better for the parents to escort both bride and groom or for the couple to enter together and the families to be given an opportunity for a special blessing sometime in the service. Whoever said that a wedding required hundreds of dollars' worth of cut flowers from the local florist? Are there not better and more appropriate ways to beautify the sanctuary? Whoever said that the service was to be as short as possible and that the congregation should not be involved? By far the most meaningful weddings in which we have participated have been those in which the congregation sang and prayed together and even danced together. Whoever said that the appropriate name for the new couple to take was Mr. and Mrs. Husband's Name? This is another tradition that goes against the basic value of equality that leads to wholeness.

As couples consider these questions, they need to feel that

they have some control over their service. This may occasionally mean that a pastor must compromise his or her own values. An alternative, of course, is not to perform the service for a couple that is intent on a service and a life-style antithetical to the pastor's.

Time and again we have counseled with young couples who are convinced they want to do something special in their wedding because that is what so and so did at theirs. Weddings are important models for others to see, and they can be examples of wholeness in worship.

HEALING SERVICES

For many years we dismissed healing services as something done only by the radical fringe of Christianity that had no positive value and often took advantage of needy people in cruel ways. We have had to do an about-face in this area.

We began to realize that our opinion had been influenced by rather flamboyant TV evangelists. We were generally so offended by their theology and methods that we dismissed the whole idea of healing. As we started reading extensively in the area of wholistic health, we began to see how closely mind and body are linked in healing and illness. We began to read of sincere, thoughtful Christians who had been practicing healing for years, people such as Agnes Sanford,[2] the Worralls,[3] and Morton Kelsey.[4] We also reread the New Testament. We were overwhelmed by the amount of healing recorded in this book and became convinced that such healing is still possible today.

The services we (mostly Sharon) have conducted during the past year or so have been modeled to some extent after those conducted by Olga Worrall. They are quiet, simple, dignified. A complete model of such a service is included in chapter 12. It is only a model that can be adapted as needed.

Healing can and does occur in "regular" worship services. It is important, however, to provide a special time and place where those who really want to pursue this concern in depth can come together. The laying-on-of-hands by the whole gath-

ered group can also be important. For this reason, a small committed group is preferable to a larger, less convinced group.
Healing services, among other things, are a visible affirmation
of the wholeness (body, mind, and spirit) of the human being.
They are a way of taking the physical body seriously in worship
as Jesus did in his ministry.

When we first began to conduct healing services we felt a
bit foolish. Who were we to try such a thing? But we felt called
to begin this ministry because of the real needs we saw about
us and felt within us. We are still novices in this area, but we
are convinced that even the most fumbling efforts can be used
by God.

FUNERALS

Funeral services are referred to in different traditions at
different times as either "The Order for the Burial of the Dead"
or as "A Witness to the Resurrection." In this case a title tells
a great deal. Is the primary purpose of a funeral to bury a
particular dead person or is it to proclaim the power of the
resurrection in the midst of grief? The funeral does achieve the
practical purpose of burying a body, but the prime purpose of
a funeral is to witness to our faith, and especially to our faith
in the resurrection. It is a service therefore of hope and joy even
in the midst of pain and suffering.

The death of a church member is a call to worship. It is a
summons for those who have loved to come and hear the message of God's love afresh—to hear how this love cannot be
defeated, not even by death.

Throughout church history various tensions have developed among Christians about what is appropriate at a Christian
funeral. Many authors have spent much time proclaiming that
either one or the other action must be done. We feel that wholistic worship's emphasis on the possibility of "both and"
rather than "either or" can be helpful here. In every case we can
see real value to both sides of these tensions.

First is the tension between the Hebraic concept of the

resurrection of the body and the Greek concept of immortality. During much of the recent past biblical scholars and others have emphasized the significance of the Hebrew concept in which the resurrection of the body is just as much a miracle as was the creation. It is the act of God defeating the natural order of death. Certainly this concept has powerful biblical justification although the Greek concept of immortality can also be found in the Bible, especially in the gospel of John. Recent psychical research on persons who have experienced "near death," however, seems to lend weight to the understanding that the soul does not perish in death but somehow lives on (the Greek concept of immortality). We believe it is time to admit an honest agnosticism about the nature of life after death and simply affirm its reality, rather than argue about how it can happen. We feel it is especially important to present this kind of positive faith at funerals. It is far preferable to a long and perhaps even erroneous theological discourse.

The second tension is that between eulogy and faith affirmation. It has been popular of late to disparage any eulogy for the desceased and concentrate instead in the funeral sermon on a faith affirmation. Eulogies can and have gotten out of hand. The primary emphasis in the funeral sermon as in the service is on a witness of faith. However, in a funeral service for a particular human being who lived in a particular way, it is appropriate to recognize the beauty of his or her life. This can be done simply, without rhetoric, either by the minister or by one or two close friends of the deceased.

A third tension is between individual solace and community affirmation. The funeral is a natural conclusion to baptism —dying and rising with Christ. It is also a beautiful time for communion, when the community shares in portraying God's love. The service needs to be pointed toward faith affirmation and therefore provide opportunities for the community as a whole to express itself through hymns and prayers. The service can also be a time for individual solace. Members of the family should be helped to choose passages of Scripture and hymns that were especially meaningful to the deceased. Periods of silence and music and dance can also provide opportunity for individual reflection and meditation.

A fourth tension concerns the funeral for the non-Christian: Should the pastor conduct it or not? Many pastors do not perform a Christian ceremony, such as a funeral, for a non-Christian. They base this position on a theology that argues for the exclusivism of the Christian faith. One of the premises of wholeness in worship is the inclusiveness of the faith. Since God's love does not cease just because someone has not yet recognized it, a Christian service affirming God's love for all humanity is appropriate even for a non-Christian.

As with the other special services, education is important if the funeral is to have the most meaning for those involved. Each church should have an ongoing program of death education in which members are encouraged to talk openly about their death and the plans they want to make for it. If such careful thought comes before the experience, friends and relatives will be much more likely to carry out a funeral that is both what the individual would have desired and (because of this) what is most meaningful to those who remain. Thought beforehand can help prevent emotional decisions made on the basis of "this is what we ought to do"; the funeral can become a celebration of the wholeness of God's unfailing love.

12

Sample Services

HERE ARE some examples of what we feel constitutes whole-ness in worship, although no single service can ever be abso-lutely whole. The services that follow contain many of the elements of wholistic worship that we have discussed.

Where it seemed sensible, we have presented only the part of the service that demonstrates a particular example. Included are five complete Sunday morning services, two complete family liturgies, a wedding service, a funeral service, and more abbreviated versions of healing, baptism, and guided imagery services.

Our purpose is not to give you something to copy word for word in your own setting but to spark your imagination so that taking an idea here and some words there, you can create ser-vices that are wholistic for your congregation.

The music comes primarily from the hymnal *Sisters and Brothers, Sing!*[1] In two cases we wanted to share with you a song not easily available, so we have reprinted it. If you wish to reproduce these songs, you will need to contact the copyright owners for permission.

Our hope is that these examples are just a beginning. We would be delighted to hear from you ways in which you have developed wholistic worship, either using some of these ser-vices in part or something you have developed. You can contact us at the Wesley Foundation, 211 North School Street, Normal, Illinois 61761.

THE EMPTY SPACE
(*A Sunday Service*)

Worship Setting: The communion table is placed down close to the congregation. On it is a small transparent abstract figure made from clear plastic bags. You should have hidden, ready to hold up, a cardboard rainbow. You will also need communion elements—a whole loaf of unsliced bread and wine or grape juice (to be brought to the table by members of the congregation at the appropriate time) and some perfume in several containers (to be used during the Words of Assurance).

Prelude: Bright, joyful music, preferably instrumental.

Hymn: "All God's Children" (p. 1*), or another hymn that emphasizes the inclusiveness of God's family. Introduce this hymn as the Call to Worship.

Call to Confession: The worship leader invites people to get in touch with themselves and asks what they feel are some of the empty spaces in their lives. The leader points out that not all emptiness is bad, but that being unable to love, unable to take time for oneself, and unable to reach out to certain other persons can be profoundly troubling emptinesses. Give the congregation time to ponder such emptinesses in themselves for a few minutes in complete silence.

Shared Confession: Invite the congregation to pair off and share, as they feel comfortable, some of the emptiness they feel in their lives. Encourage them to see this as a confession shared with a priest: all of us are part of the priesthood of all believers. Allow enough time for this sharing to happen in some depth, but when you sense that most persons are finished, call the group back together.

Words of Assurance:
LEADER: God's love helps us to begin to fill our emptiness. It

*Page number refers to Tom Neufer Emswiler and Sharon Neufer Emswiler, eds., *Sisters and Brothers, Sing!* You may substitute hymns from your congregation's hymnal.

is through this love that we have the courage to keep going and the hope that our future contains new possibilities of joyful fulfillment. One of the ways Christians have symbolized the power of God's love for our lives has been through the use of perfume—the sweet fragrance of God. Just as a few minutes ago you shared confession with one another, we invite you to share assurance together. We ask that one of you cup your hands as a sign of your emptiness. The other will then anoint those hands with perfume as a sign of God's powerful love at work in your life. Then you will simply exchange roles and repeat the act. While this is happening, those not immediately involved in anointing and those already finished will sing the hymn "Matthew 11:28–30" (p. 59).

Scripture Readings:

Romans 12:1–2: I appeal to you, friends, to give your whole selves to God; body, mind, and spirit. Thus you become a living sacrifice, fully acceptable to God through your expression of wholistic worship. Don't let the world determine your behavior, but instead let God help you be transformed so that you will be able to know God's will, that is, what is good, right, and perfect. (Paraphrase by Tom and Sharon Neufer Emswiler.)

Luke 15:1–8: The tax collectors and other bad characters were all crowding around Jesus to listen to him; and they began grumbling to themselves: "This guy welcomes sinners and eats with them." Jesus heard them and answered with these parables. "Who among you with a hundred sheep and losing one of them does not leave the ninety-nine in the open pasture and go after the missing one until it is found? How delighted you are then, and you go home and call your friends and neighbors together saying, 'Rejoice with me. I have found my lost sheep.' I tell you, in the same way there will be greater joy in heaven over one sinner who repents than over ninety-nine righteous people who do not need to repent. Or again, if you have ten silver coins and lose one of them, don't you light the lamp, sweep out the house, and look in

every nook and cranny until you have found it? And when
it is found you say, 'Rejoice with me! I have found the coin
that I lost.' In the same way, there is joy among God's angels
over one sinner who repents."

"And who among you losing a contact lens does not gather
family and friends around until that which was lost is found?
And having found it rejoice in again being able to see. In the
same way, there is joy in heaven over one sinner who repents."[2]

Sermon: "The Empty Space: A Fable." For this dialogue sermon between a man and a woman you will need the abstract
figure and rainbow described in "Worship Setting." After the
parable is enacted, the ideas listed at the conclusion of this
parable may be shared in a dialogue.[3]

1:   It was empty.
2:   It had been at least partly empty all of its life.
1:   And for as long as it could remember, it had been search-
      ing for something to fill the emptiness.
2:   The search was kind of fun.
1:   It would go here.
2:   It would go there.
1:   Climbing mountains
2:   Sliding down into lovely valleys
1:   And as it went it would sing
2:   "Oh golly ho
      Here I go
      Trying to be filled
      Up and down
      All around
      I never seem to succeed."
1:   It really needed a word to rhyme with "filled"
2:   But it could never think of one, so it just used "succeed."
1:   Still the journey was a pleasant adventure
2:   Especially nice in the friendly sun.
1:   It would take time to stretch out and let the sun caress
      its body.

2: Sometimes a little breeze would come

1: And blow a beautiful leaf right onto its stomach.

2: Other times a bird would take courage and come close to it and they would talk and chirp for hours.

1: Sometimes it got cold

2: But it had friends with nice fur coats who could help it.

1: Or it got real hot

2: But then a cool rain would come.

1: And sometimes the sun would keep on shining right during the rain.

2: This was the best time of all [A rainbow appears—make one out of cardboard.]

1: Day after day passed.

2: And it kept on searching.

1: It found some great things.

2: But everytime it got something really nice

1: Like a friend

2: Or money

1: Or knowledge

2: Or sex

1: Or fame

2: It still felt some emptiness. The things it found filled somewhat, but never completely.

1: Until ...

2: One day it encountered religion.

1: This particular religion claimed to have all the answers

2: And it swallowed the religion hook, line, and Bible.

1: And for once, it was full.

2: "Oh wow, I'm full" shouted it.

1: It was so happy that it did a little song and dance right there.

2: "Oh golly ho
Here I go" [sing very slowly and slurred]

1: "Oh, oh. Something is wrong here," thought it. I'm so full I can't sing, and there is no way I'm going to be able to dance."

2: So very carefully
1: It put back this particular brand of religion.
2: It put it back hook, line,
1: And Bible.
2: And then it could sing and dance again.
       "Oh golly ho
       Here I go
       Trying to be filled
       Up and down
       All around
       I never seem to succeed."
1: As it sang and danced a light rain began to fall,
2: But the sun kept on shining.
1: And it stood still and just enjoyed the promise in the sky.

Most worship services contain a number of empty spaces. If some of these spaces were somehow filled in, worship would have much greater wholeness. These empty spaces include the following:

1. Recognition of the body
    Our Scripture from Romans tells us that we are to present our bodies, in fact our whole beings, to God in worship. Unfortunately, we usually present only a portion of our minds. This has not always been so. Share with your congregation some of the history of dance in the church (see pp.61–62). If you dare, invite them to join you in doing the tripudium. Mention other ways of involving the body in worship—gestures, processions, and so on.

2. Touch
    Touch is the language of love, but in many worship services we never touch another human being. Our society is inhibited because of the sexual implications of touch, but we all have hungers for touch that supersede sexual needs. Share with people the history of the "kiss of peace." Ask, "What better place for reaching out and touching another human being than in church?"

3. Interaction among members of the congregation

   Unfortunately, one can attend a service and not speak to another soul. When the members of the body of Christ won't have anything to do with one another, we're in trouble.

4. Involvement of women

   Even though the majority in most congregations is women, one often sees no women in leadership roles in worship. They are also excluded through the use of male generic language and masculine concepts of God. If we are concerned about the whole body of Christ, this must change.

5. Silence

   We seem to be afraid of silence. In worship the richness of quiet is not a part of our celebrations. Do we fear silence because a void in us cannot creatively use such a time? We need to allow for periods of silence in our services.

There are many other empty spaces in worship. Attempting to obtain wholeness in worship is an adventure that will never be fully completed. In fact, if we think we have everything together, then we have probably closed ourselves up to God's surprises and God's promises. The rainbow should remind us that there is always more to God than we can grasp. There is also more to worship than we can ever achieve. But we can make giant strides toward filling some of the emptiness of most modern worship. As we do this we will become much more in tune with the power of God's love for our lives.

Offering: Of money
          Of our joys and concerns

Communion: Persons in the congregation bring the elements forward and place them on the communion table.

MINISTER (lifting the elements): The gifts of God for the people of God.
CONGREGATION: Amen.

MINISTER: These elements symbolize our creative powers. It
is no mean task to create bread and wine. On this table
these elements are transformed into expressions of Jesus
Christ. The bread is broken into pieces. The wine is spilled.
When we gather about this table, the body is put back
together again, this time in us. Our most powerful statement of wholism may come at times when we the committed, loving people gather to let the pieces of Christ be
reassembled in us.

On the same night that Christ was betrayed, he took
bread and broke it and said, "This is my body broken for
you." Eat this that you might be whole.

Likewise he took the cup, and he said "This cup is my
blood of the new covenant shed for you and for many for
the forgiveness of sin." Drink this that your lives may be
transfused with the eternal life of Christ's love.

(The congregation gathers around the communion table
and takes the elements in a big circle, if possible. Joyful music
can be played or sung at this time.)

Prayer of Thanksgiving: You have taken the scattered pieces
of our lives and bound them together in your love, O God,
and we are thankful. We are amazed by the promise and
power your love gives our lives. We are fed and ready to be
your body in the world. Amen.

Hymn: "One but Not the Same" (p. 107), or another hymn
that emphasizes both the diversity and the unity found in the
Christian faith.˙

Benediction: "Shalom." The minister explains the meaning
of this Old Testament concept. It means much more than
"peace," as it is usually translated. It means wholeness,
maturity, all the best for humanity that can be dreamed. The
congregation is then invited to sing the folk song "Shalom"
(see p. 125 for the music, although we use different words
here) and to do the following simple movements with partners:

Words	Actions
Shalom, my friend	Partners face each other and place right hands together at about shoulder or face level.
Shalom, my friend	Still touching right hands, partners touch left hands so that the arms are now crossed.
Shalom, shalom	Partners grasp hands in same position and raise above heads, looking upward.
May Christ be with you	Partners embrace lightly, placing right sides of face together,
May Christ be with you	then left sides together.
Shalom	Each places own hands in traditional praying gesture, palms together, fingers pointing upward. One partner places his or her hands over that of the other.
Shalom	No longer touching hands, each bows to the other with hands still in praying gesture, as in the Oriental custom of bowing to the presence of Christ in the neighbor.

IMAGING GOD
(*A Sunday Service*)

God's image is not limited to one place, one time, one religion, or one person. Rather it pervades the universe from the tiniest atom to the highest mountain. God is all and yet beyond all that we know. As Christians we affirm that this all embracing power is love.

Prelude: Gentle, quiet music

Call to Worship: Scholars tell us that the word *God* is probably derived from the original Indo-Germanic word *ghu-to,* "the called one" or "the one who is called." We are here because in some way or other we have felt the call of this one we have named God, but some other names are more descriptive of our God. Let us now call forth some of these names. Write in your bulletin one name for God that is important and meaningful for you. Then I will invite you to call out these words as our Call to Worship.

Hymn: "My Name" (p. 80), or another hymn that includes a number of different names for God.

A Time of Greeting: If you were to meet God face-to-face, what would you say? In a sense we meet God every time we meet one another; we are "in God's image." Through people we experience the personal reality of God. Let us greet one another in reverence.

Call to Confession: Made "in God's image," all of us have fallen dramatically. God's image of self-giving love has been marred and blurred in the dungeons of evil. We come therefore in humility to confess our fallenness and to ask God's help in picking up the pieces of our lives.

General Prayer of Confession: O God, you are like a father who passionately cares for the welfare of his family. You have strength, integrity, and gentle love to pour out upon us, but we often sabotage your hopes for us. We abuse our minds and bodies, and we fail to live with discipline and therefore waste hours of precious time on activities that are neither beneficial nor fun. Help us to care for ourselves and one another in the way in which you call us to be the best we can be.

O God, you are like a mother who tenderly, yet powerfully, reaches out to weave the fabric of love into all relationships. We are guilty of rending that fabric through insensitivity, jealousy, and selfishness. We have used others for our own pleasures and goals. Help us, like you, to become weavers of the strong, gentle love that makes the difference between existing and living a life of abundance. In the name of Jesus we pray, Amen.

Words of Assurance: Most parents will love their children no matter what; God is like that, but much more. God's word to you today is, "Nothing you can do will make me stop loving you. Arise, pick up your life and walk!"

Scripture Readings: These readings have been chosen because they image God in "feminine" ways that we usually overlook.

Isaiah 49:14–16.   Follow this reading with the hymn "I Will not Forget You" (p. 60), or another hymn that refers to God in feminine terms.

Matthew 23:37
Luke 15:8–10

Sermon: *The Vision,* a film written and produced by Sharon and Tom Neufer Emswiler; animator, Sam Klemke; available from Mass Media Ministries, 2116 N. Charles St., Baltimore, Maryland 21218. This film comes with a complete discussion guide, from which you can get ideas for involving your congregation in responding to it and to the general idea of expanding one's images of God. At some place in the discussion, the song "Father Me, Mother Me" by Marita Brake, found at the end of this service, can be shared. If you reproduce the song, you will need to contact the composer to do so. The purpose of this sermon is to help people become aware of the exciting possibilities of seeing God in different images.

Announcements and Sharing of Joys and Concerns

Offering: A sharing of money and bringing forth of the communion elements.

Taking the Bread and Cup:
LEADER: The gifts of God for the people of God.
CONGREGATION: Amen.

The Great Thanksgiving:
LEADER: It is good, O God, that you come to us in a thousand guises, stirring our hearts and minds with the fullness of your being. It is good too that you shared yourself with us most especially in the humanity of Jesus. Through this incredible act of humbling yourself we have come to see most clearly how much you love us.

CONGREGATION: Our minds cannot get around such love; our hearts cannot hold it all. We stand before you, God, in grateful adoration.

LEADER: And we remember the way in which this love was finally fully manifested in a simple supper Jesus had with the disciples. Jesus knew what lay ahead, and he wanted to find the most vivid means possible of sharing all he was with the disciples. He seized upon the Jewish Feast of Liberation, celebrating the freedom of the Hebrews from slavery, and he extended it to include all people and to be embodied in him. He took bread and broke it, and later his disciples remembered this brokenness when his body was torn on the cross and again after the resurrection as he shared a meal with some of them. He took the cup and told them that it was his blood spilled for them and for many. On the cross they saw it pouring from his wounds. In the years to come they knew its power for cleansing them and all sinners.

CONGREGATION: God, you died for us. The power of this changes us, transforms us again and again.

LEADER: We know, God, that your spirit is with us today, blessing this time and these elements. We pray that its power can infuse us as we receive these elements and that it can help us bring healing and justice to our world.

CONGREGATION: You have said it for us all. Alleluia! Amen.

Sharing Communion: This should be done in whatever manner seems best for your congregation. We would hope this would include congregational movement of some kind and a common loaf and cup. Perhaps the songs used in the service as hymns could be sung gently by a soloist while communion is being received.

Hymn: "Who Knows the Face of God" (p. 76), or another hymn that includes a balance of both masculine and feminine images for God.

A Navajo Benediction (Prayed together):

God is before us.
God is behind us.
God is above us.
God is below us.
God's words shall come from our mouths.
For we are God's essence, a sign of God's love.
All is finished in beauty
All is finished in beauty
All is finished in beauty
All is finished in beauty.[4]

Father Me, Mother Me

Words and Music by
Marita Brake

Refrain

Fa - ther me,___ moth - er me,___ so all my sis - ters and

broth - ers see___ your good - ness and your kind - ness, and the

love you've got to give is for - ev - er time - less.___

1. When I'm down I need a Fa - ther to help me through the
2. You are sure - ly my heav'n - ly fa - ther and you re - mind me of a
3. I'm your prod - i - gal daugh - ter and way - ward son___ and I'm feel - ing like my

things that both - er me;___ when I'm sick I
brood - ing moth - er hen;___ so hold me close, spread your
life has just___ be - gun;___ so let me sit down___

need a moth - er to nurse me back and help me re - dis - cov - er
wings a - round___ me, keep me here and let your love sur - round me a -
on your knee,___ hold my hand and keep me com - pa - ny___ till

thee.___
gain.___
then.___

THE RHYTHM OF GOD
(A Sunday Service)

The worship center could include a cross, a ticking clock, a stethoscope, some drums, and other rhythm instruments. If drums are brought, a person should be prepared to play them. Begin the service by reading Ecclesiastes 3;1–8, or ask someone to sing Pete Seeger's version of this scripture. The reading or singing might be done from the back of the church.

Call to Worship:
LEADER: It is time to worship now.

CONGREGATION: We have taken time in our busy schedules to come and honor God.

LEADER: And God returns the honor. The rhythm God set loose in the heart of the universe is beating in you.

CONGREGATION: We are here today to try to get in touch with this rhythm. It is our source of aliveness, our gateway to fulfilled living.

LEADER: Let your love beat in us, O God, until we all begin moving to your time.

CONGREGATION: Amen.

Hymn: "Take Time" (p. 153): the drummer can accompany this song—as it ends, he or she can continue the slow incessant beat for a couple of minutes and then build into a crescendo of rhythm and sound; or another hymn about time that has a strong and interesting rhythmic beat.

Call to Confession: Sometimes we are like that drumbeat. We move from listless steadiness into enthusiastic abandon, or we move from the ordered beat of regularity into a chaos of uncertainty. Let us admit the ways we are sometimes out of rhythm. (Invite people to turn to their neighbors and share some of the problems they have with time—wasting it, for example, or being too frantic or too calculated about it. After a few minutes call the group back together and invite them to share in the general prayer of confession.

General Prayer of Confession: God, we are often out of
rhythm with ourselves, one another, and you. Our lives demand a variety of rhythms to grow in creativity and love, but
sometimes our varieties become hurtful chaos. We often get
ourselves on treadmills and do not have time to enjoy the
wonder of life. Help us slow down, God, and appreciate the
marvelous gifts we have. We sometimes get so set in certain
rhythms, certain patterns, that we are blind to new possibilities. Open our eyes, God, and help us to see fresh opportunities through you. We rush headlong into areas we think we
should pursue to become rich or famous or well liked, and
suddenly we realize we have entirely left out time for you.
Help us, God, to reevaluate our priorities. In Christ's name we
pray, Amen.

Words of Assurance: Be quiet for a few minutes and get in
touch with your breathing. God gave you breath. It is God's
spirit within you. Knowing this, how can you doubt that God
is with you? Simply stop and pay attention to your breathing.
It is God's way of saying "I love you" over and over again.

Hymn: "Peace Time" (p. 75): use drums to accompany the
hymn, and encourage the congregation to become their own
rhythm instruments by clapping their hands, snapping their
fingers, stomping their feet—most likely you or a choir will
need to lead in these actions; or another rhythmic hymn
about the Beautitudes.

Scripture Readings:
Mark 1:14–15
Romans 8:18–27

Sermon: "The Rhythm of God." This sermon could concentrate on the ways in which God's time is both like and unlike
ours. It could make use of insights shared in this book in the
section on rhythm (see pp.14–17). The whole universe may
be yearning to get into entrainment with God, into basic
rhythm with the creator of the universe. This is what Paul

was getting at in the Romans 8:18 ff. passage. There is also the "right time" for God and for us as human beings. This moment was expressed in the coming of Jesus, but it can be repeated in our own lives at moments of crisis and important decisions. At the same time, in some ways God's sense of time must be vastly different from ours. You may want to share the old joke that goes something like this:

"What does a billion dollars mean to you, God? You are all-powerful, so it must not mean much," said the man.
"Hardly a penny," God answered.
"And what are a hundred thousand centuries?"
"Hardly a second."
"Then, O God, give me a penny," begged the man.
"In a second."

Questions about the judgment of God, the discernment of God, and so on must be weighed against our vague understanding that time is much different for the creator of the universe. Perhaps we have often misunderstood God because we have not allowed him and her to be in a totally different time dimension.

Hymn: "Live into Hope" (p. 90), or another hymn about Christian hope.

A Sharing of Time with Your Brothers and Sisters: Invite an informal sharing of joys and concerns with time afterward for quiet prayers about them.

Offering: Encourage people not only to give of their money, which is their time wrapped in paper or gold, but also to take time to rededicate themselves to living as they feel God wants them to. Ask them to place their right hands on the left side of their chest and feel the steady rhythm of their hearts. As the offering plate or basket comes to them, invite them to take their right hands and slowly place them into the basket as if the hand still held their beating heart. Ask them to leave the hand in the basket until they have completed a silent prayer of dedication to God. They are then to put their monetary offering into the plate and pass it on to the next person.

Act of Dedication:

LEADER: Time is a fragment of eternity.

CONGREGATION: It is the most precious gift we can give each other.

LEADER: Time to listen.

CONGREGATION: Time to comfort and be comforted.

LEADER: Time to cultivate fragile relationships.

CONGREGATION: Into durable eternal friendships.

LEADER: Time to risk rejection.

CONGREGATION: Time for silence.

LEADER: Time to share our faith.

CONGREGATION: We dedicate ourselves to use the precious gift of time with the carefulness we have just described. We have time, God. Help us to use it lovingly. Amen.[6]

Benediction: "Go Gently through the Years" (p. 126), or another blessing song with a time dimension.

CASTING OUT OUR FEARS
(A Sunday Service)

Worship Setting: The worship table should be in the midst of the people if possible. On it should be various symbols of fear, such as a gun, a mushroom (nuclear destruction), an ambulance, a clock. Also on the table should be a butterfly candle, symbolizing hope and the light of the world, and a loaf of bread and a chalice of wine for communion, representing God's love for us.

Prelude: Calming music

Call to Worship:
FIRST LEADER: Fear not, little flock, for it is God's good pleasure to give you all that you need [based on Luke 12:32].
SECOND LEADER: Fear not? You've got to be kidding. In the last few months here in [name your town or area] we have had [name some of the things that have happened—rapes, knifings, shootings, robberies, and so on]. Do you mean to tell me I shouldn't be afraid?
FIRST LEADER: "In God I trust without a fear. What can flesh do to me?" [Psalm 56:4].
SECOND LEADER: For one thing it can kill you. For another it can torture you and maim you horribly. You've got to be out of your mind not to fear in today's world.
FIRST AND SECOND LEADERS: And so we come to worship to consider a central issue in our lives. How can we handle our fears?

Hymn: "Hide Me" (p. 133), or another song using this image from the Psalms of being hidden by God.

A Time of Confession:
FIRST LEADER: One way we often want to react to fear is to hide. This is not always a stupid response; it can save our lives. But if we always hide in the face of fear, we become

afraid ever to take risks. We prefer to hide in the safety of jobs we know how to do, people with whom we feel comfortable, situations which we know we can handle. Have you been hiding? How? This is your time to share with God some of the ways you've been hiding from the person you know you should be and what you know you should do.

(A quiet time for individual prayer)

Words of Assurance:

SECOND LEADER: But to hide in the shadow of God's wings may mean something different. Could it refer to our admitting our need for help beyond ourselves? Could it be a beginning of learning how to deal with our fears? No matter how dangerous the situation, God never deserts us. Those are the words of real assurance.

Hymn: "Jesus, Jesus" (p. 40), or another simple round about Jesus' love for each of us.

A Fantasy Experience: We can only begin to deal with something when we have owned it. We have to admit that it is a part of us, touching our lives, affecting our actions. As we consider fear, I invite you to get in touch with a fear you have. It may be something silly that has bothered you for years, or it may be something so deep and pervasive that you don't even have words for it. You can get as far into this fear as you want. No one will force you to go more deeply than you are able.

Get comfortable, and if it feels right, close your eyes. Try to imagine the thing you fear most. Perhaps it's being killed in a traffic accident; maybe it's being rejected by someone you love; possibly it's losing your job or flunking out of school. Whatever it is, begin to imagine it. If possible, actually feel this fear with your body. Let it rest there for a moment [long pause]. The uneasiness, the pain you may be feeling right now is what we will deal with in this service. Now, take this feeling you have and gently place it on a shelf in one of

your closets at home or at work. We'll come back to it, but
for now we can shelve it and rejoin everyone in this room.

Scripture Reading:

Old Testament: Isaiah 35:1–4

LEFT: The wilderness and the dry land shall be glad,
the desert shall rejoice and bloom,

RIGHT: It shall bloom forth with wild flowers,
with bright jonquils.

LEFT: It shall sing and shout for joy.

RIGHT: The desert will be as glorious as Lebanon,
its splendor like the fertile fields
of Carmel and Sharon.

LEFT: Everyone shall see God's glory,
the splendor of our Creator.

RIGHT: Give strength to tired hands,
steady all trembling knees,

LEFT: Tell those who are downhearted,
"Have courage! Don't be afraid.

RIGHT: God is coming to your rescue
and your enemies will not overtake you."[7]

New Testament: 1 John 4:7–12, 16–21

LEADER: Dear friends, let us love one another, for love
comes straight from God.

CONGREGATION: For those who love are God's children and
know God.

LEADER: God's love was manifested among us when God
sent Jesus into the world so that we might discover the
meaning of life through Christ.

CONGREGATION: God's love is primary. All love flows from
the truth of God's love in Christ. This love has the power
to bring forgiveness to us all.

LEADER: Friends, if this is how God loved us, then we
should love one another in the same way.

CONGREGATION: No one has ever seen God, but if we love

one another, God lives in us and Christ's love is made
perfect in us.

LEADER: God is love; those who live in love live in God and
God lives in them.

CONGREGATION: Thus we have courage as we face the judgment, because our life in this world is strengthened by
Christ.

LEADER: There is no fear in love; perfect love drives out all
fear. Fear is brought about by punishment, but if we are
perfected in love, we no longer worry about punishment.

CONGREGATION: We love because God first loved us.

LEADER: If anyone says, "I love God," but hates sister or
brother, that person is a liar.

CONGREGATION: If we do not love our sister or brother
whom we see, we cannot love God whom we do not see.
This, then, is the commandment Christ gave us: We who
love God must love our sisters and brothers too.[8]

Sermon Fantasy Experience: "Casting Out All Fear." This
sermon makes use of a technique described by Dennis and
Matthew Linn in their book *Healing Life's Hurts: Healing
Memories through the Five Stages of Forgiveness.*[9] Called
"adopting the Christ model," this technique involves the
following stages:

1.   Recognize that Jesus also experienced fear. He does truly
go before us in life's problems. Reflect on the fear Jesus
must have felt as he prayed in Gethsemane with such
anguish that sweat poured from him like great drops of
blood (Luke 22:42).

2.   What can we learn from Jesus' experience with fear? He
knew the two basic ways of handling fear—removing it
or going through it. In Gethsemane he prayed for his fear
to be removed. Although it did not happen then, sometimes this is a solution. Jesus did chase Satan away in the
desert. In Gethsemane Jesus finally had to live through
his fear, discovering growth and power by facing the fear
head on and going through it with God's help.

3. With this background we may now go back to our fantasy of a few minutes ago. Take your fear down off the closet shelf, and tell Jesus all about it. Describe it so fully that you again begin to feel it bodily.

4. Watch Jesus react to your fear. Is he helping you remove it, chase it away, or is he saying that you must go through it with God's help?

You may want to conclude this sermon by breaking into small groups (triads) and inviting people to share what they want with one another about their fears and what they are beginning to understand Christ wants done about them. Or you may wish to conclude by sharing with the congregation some of your own fears and how you have used this method to come to new understandings and growth concerning them.

A Song of Courage: "A Better Country" (p. 110), or another song that emphasizes our need to model our lives after those of courageous Christians who have gone before us.

Sharing Announcements, Joys, and Concerns

Offering: Giving God our fears as well as our money.

Communion: If your setting allows, take communion with everyone standing in one big circle. If this is not possible, share communion with the people coming forward to receive it at designated stations about the church.

The Eucharistic Prayer:

LEADER: O God, you mothered and fathered us, and we know that you care for us with a love deeper than any human parent.

CONGREGATION: And so we come to you in great rejoicing, knowing that whatever our fears may be, you are greater than they are.

LEADER: We remember the fears of the Hebrew people as they faced bondage and then the uncertainty of freedom.

CONGREGATION: You were with them day and night. You never forsake us.

LEADER: We remember the fears of Jesus as he faced the torment of the cross.

CONGREGATION: You stood by him in heartbroken love. You stand with us even when we break your heart.

LEADER: We remember the fear and confusion of the disciples after the horror of the crucifixion.

CONGREGATION: And you answered their fears in the glorious power of the resurrection. You still rebirth us today.

LEADER: And so we stand in God's spirit today as we remember again how Christ stood with the disciples taking a loaf of bread, lifting it for all to see, and saying, "This is my body, broken [break loaf] for you. Eat this in remembrance of me."

CONGREGATION:.   You have been broken that we might be whole.

LEADER: In the same manner Christ took the cup, lifted it [lift cup], and said, "This cup is the new covenant of my blood spilled for you and for many for the forgiveness of sin. Drink this, all of you, in remembrance of me."

CONGREGATION: Your blood was shed that we might be transfused with God's love.

LEADER: As we share in this communion today, we know that we share with the whole host of heaven. We pause now in thanks for those both living and dead who have shared their love and faith with us; let us name them joyfully in our hearts. We come to take these elements in the firm knowledge that this is the best medicine for fear. God's spirit is with us, helping us receive in special power the strong love of God.

As communion is shared, reflective music should be played or sung, either by a soloist, the choir, or the congregation as a whole.

Prayer of Thanksgiving: Thank you, God, for being with us when we're afraid. Thank you for coming here and knowing the taste of fear. Thank you for standing by us when we need you so much. Your love that is in us and around us helps us cast out our fears so that we can rejoice in life's great beauties. Amen.

Benediction: "A Circle of Love," sung to the tune of "May the Circle Be Unbroken," in a circle if possible.

> May the circle be unbroken
> Through your love that we share here.
> May the circle be unbroken
> Through your love that we share here.
>
> May we live lives freed from fear now
> As we journey on our way.
> May we live lives freed from fear now
> As we journey on our way.

BEING LIKE A CHILD
(*A Sunday Service*)

This service makes use of the storytelling model. The stories are from personal experiences or from the book *The Ministry of the Child* by Dennis C. Benson and Stan J. Steward. The stories from Benson and Steward's book are summarized. We encourage you to substitute stories from your own experience.

Worship Setting: The worship table is set for a feast. The food should look inviting, contrasting in shape, color, texture, and flavor. Avoid food that might be dangerous to small children, such as nuts. Include items such as marshmallows, chocolates, cookies, apples, and green grapes. Drape some soft, fresh-smelling baby blankets over the table to one side. Have one blanket for every ten participants in the service.

Prelude: Bright, happy music

Call to Worship:
  LEADER: Jesus did not say that we should be like the president of the United States or the head of a large business corporation.
  CONGREGATION: He said instead that we should be like a little child.
  LEADER: And so we come together now to learn from children.
  CONGREGATION: May our spirits be led to deeper understanding of God as we listen to the wisdom of children.

Hymn: "Everybody Has a Song" (p. 132), or another hymn that emphasizes the unique gifts each of us has to offer.

A Reflection: Everybody does have a song. Whenever our young son is especially happy, he sings spontaneously. We know when he really likes his food because he hums while he eats. Most of us are not professional singers, but something in our hearts makes us sing. Discovering what we sing about and then sharing that song with others is one of the most important things we can do in our lives. What do you sing about? How are you sharing this song?

Call to Confession: *The Story of Ted.* When I [Tom] was a little boy, I ran with a gang of boys at recess. We liked to chase Ted, the class outcast. Ted always wore old patched clothes. He stuttered, he often didn't smell good, and he was not very smart in class. The other boys chased him and called him names. One day we caught him, and, not knowing what else to do, we started to beat him up. The teacher saw what was happening and came running over, grabbed the crying Ted up in her arms, and took him inside. Later she gave the rest of us boys the talking to of our lives. For the first time I began to realize that people much different from me had feelings and could be desperately hurt. I began to see my own involvement in the reality of sin. Most of us haven't beaten up little kids lately, but we may have hurt someone in other ways through an unkind word, by ignoring someone, by making fun of another, or passing along malicious gossip. In the time that follows I invite you to make your own prayer of confession to God for ways in which you have hurt others.

Quiet Prayers of Confession

Words of Assurance: *Sharing Baby Blankets.* All of us have probably been comforted at some time in our lives by the softness of a blanket. Just the touch and smell of a fresh clean baby blanket often stirs up memories within us. At this time we ask you to come and get a blanket from the worship table and share it in groups of ten. Pass it around, touch it, smell it. Then share with one another experiences from early childhood when you felt especially comforted. [Call people back together again.]

A student was writing a paper for a seminary class and typed, "God has taken away our quilt"—he hit a "q" rather than a "g." The professor wrote in the margin: "That's all right. God promised to send us the comforter."

My word of assurance to you is that God has indeed sent us the comforter. God's Holy Spirit is with us, helping us through whatever we face.

The Healing Touch of Children: A young preacher was trying to preach a sermon of comfort to a woman who had recently been told she had a terminal illness. Although he had worked his hardest on the sermon, he could tell he was not getting through to her. Then a little child from the back of the congregation wiggled free of his parents and walked down the aisle. He came right to where the woman was sitting and snuggled up beside her. He put his arm around her. She reached out and hugged him. After a minute the child went back to his parents, but the woman was noticeably changed. His touch had given her hope and courage.[10]

Could it be that some of the best contributions to worship by our smaller members are their interruptions?

Scripture Readings:
Matthew 18:1–6 and 19:13–15.   At that time the disciples came to Jesus and asked, "Who is the greatest in God's realm?"

Jesus asked a child to come and stand before them. "I assure you," he said, "unless you change and become like children, you will never enter the Age to Come. The greatest in God's realm are the ones who humble themselves and become like this child. Whoever welcomes in my name one such child as this, welcomes me.

"If you should cause one of these little ones to lose faith in me, it would be better that you had a large millstone tied around your neck and be drowned in the deep sea."

Some people brought children to Jesus for him to bless, but the disciples scolded the people. Jesus said, "Let the children come to me and do not stop them. The Age to Come belongs to such as these."

He placed his hands on them and then went away. (Paraphrase by Tom and Sharon Neufer Emswiler.)

Children Give Unashamedly of Themselves: A young fellow was driving an ice cream truck for the summer. On his route he stopped the same places every day to sell ice cream to the children who came flocking when they heard his bell. One day his truck would not start after he had stopped at one of his regular stations. The children were delighted that he would be with them all day, but he was upset because, as he explained to the children, he needed to finish his route and sell a lot of ice cream. He needed money to be able to go back to school in the fall and to get married. He stepped back into his truck to try to start it one more time. It seemed hopeless. Then he felt a rocking sensation from the back of the truck. He stepped from the cab and saw twenty small children trying to push the huge vehicle. Every face strained with the overwhelming task. They were determined to help their friend.[11]

Hymn: "Worries" (p. 130), or another simple children's song that points us to a stronger faith.

Offering and Announcements: Invite everyone to march up front and deposit his or her offering in the baskets on the worship table while brisk, marchlike music is playing. Let different persons from the congregation, including children, when appropriate, make the announcements.

Children Share Joys and Concerns with Us: It's not much fun to go to a circus alone, but take a little child with you, and it becomes a ball. You experience again your own first excitement and joy in a circus through the child's eyes. Sharing our joys in the church is a little like this. Through this sharing we find our joys affirmed and multiplied.

But it is equally important to share sorrows. Sorrows can overwhelm us when we are alone. When someone shares them with us, they lose their frightening power over us. An old man in a hospital waiting room was wailing and moaning in grief. The others in the room tried to be polite and leave the man to his sorrow, but a little girl toddled over to him. She reached out her hand to his face and wiped the tears from his cheeks, saying over and over again, "All right, all right, all right." The shape of the man's mouth changed slowly. He gazed at the littlest one in the room as she continued to wipe his face, and then he took her hand in his and gently kissed it.[12] That's what we attempt to do when we share concerns. We hold each other in God's love and say, "All right, all right, all right."

Sharing Joys and Concerns: If this is not a regular part of your service, you may want to ask some people ahead of time to be ready to share something. After the concerns have been shared, a time of silent prayer for them is followed either by the congregation's saying "All right, all right, all right" or a short prayer summarizing these concerns by the worship leader followed by the "All right, all right, all right." The joys could be followed by a glorious shout of "Thanks, God!" from the whole congregation.

Hymn: "Magic Penny" (p. 124), or another song that points out how we can share love with each other and how in sharing, the love increases.

A Love Feast: "Goodies" light up the eyes of the child within us. To close this service we invite everyone to come forward to the worship table. Take one item from the table and give it to someone else. Remember that a good party does not depend on how much you eat but on with whom and how you eat. As you share food with one another, we hope you'll share part of yourselves too. Did something in the service strike a special responsive chord with you? If so, share that. Share the food until it's all gone. Thank you, God, for goodies and the goodness you have shown us in this community of faith. Amen.

WIND
(*A Family Liturgy**)

Worship Setting: Fill the worship room with as many things as possible that are affected by the wind—mobiles hanging from doorways, candles burning brightly, soap bubbles, a miniature windmill, pinwheels, balloons, paper airplanes, and so on. As people gather, invite them to look around the worship room and find as many things as they can that are affected by the wind.

Call to Worship: Welcome people informally. Let them know you are glad to see them, and invite them to share some of their discoveries about the wind objects as they get introduced to one another.

Hymn: "Yes I Am" (p. 15), or another simple song of praise.

Scripture Reading:
Genesis 2:7 (read by a child, perhaps using this paraphrase by us):   Then God took some soil from the ground and formed a person out of it; God breathed life-giving breath into the person's nostrils and the person began to live.

Act of Praise: Close your eyes now and take a trip with me in your mind. Begin to breathe deeply. As you breathe in, imagine that you are bringing into your body everything good and beautiful that you can imagine. As you breathe out, imagine you are sending forth all the ugly and awful things you can imagine. Our breath is a gift from God. In Hebrew one of the words for God's spirit is the same as the word for breath. When we breathe in the freshness of new air, it is as if we were breathing in God. Now for a minute try to stop breathing all together. How long can you hold your breath? Not very long. God wants us to live. God wants us to have all that is beautiful in life. And so God created us in such a way that our bodies force us to breathe.

*Family liturgies are for the whole family of God, not just nuclear families.

Call to Confession and Quiet Individual Confession: The
wind is also known for its destructive powers and can take
the form of tornadoes and hurricanes. When the destructive
powers get hold of our lives, we sometimes feel winded,
wounded, even suffocated. Let us think about ways in which
we have been like a destructive wind, ways in which we have
hurt others.

Group Sharing about Destructive Powers Within Us

Words of Assurance: ·
Forgiveness my friend is blowing in the wind
Forgiveness is blowing in the wind
(sung to the tune of "Blowin' in the Wind").

Sermon: *Soap Bubbles, People, and God.* Blow a few soap bubbles, and then invite the congregation to reflect on the process. How are soap bubbles like people? Some possible
answers: They are all different. They are fragile and easily
broken (as are most people's feelings and dreams). They both
take breath to give them life. They are both beautiful. How
does God relate to soap bubbles and people? Some possible
responses: God created both. God feels hurt when our lives
are smashed, just as we are hurt when a beautiful soap bubble
is popped. The same gentleness and patience that it requires
to blow a beautiful bubble is also descriptive of the love God
has for us as we struggle toward new births.

Scripture Reading:
Matthew 19:13–15 (read by a child, perhaps using this paraphrase by us):   Some people brought children to Jesus for
him to place his hands on them and to pray for them, but the
disciples scolded the people. Jesus said, "Let the children
come to me and do not stop them, because the realm of
heaven belongs to such as these." He placed his hands on
them and then went away.

Reflections on This Scripture: Help the congregation to see
that God loves us and enjoys us no matter what our age.
God's spirit likes to play with us.

Hymn: "The Spirit Plays with Us" (sung to the tune of "Farmer in the Dell"). If the group is fairly small, ask them to form one large circle. If the group is large, ask them to form several smaller circles of adults and children. As the song is sung, each person gets to be in the middle of the circle and sung to, using that person's Christian name. The group sings the song through once as written and then does a stanza with each name and finally ends with the song as written. A simple dance step or skip around the person in the middle of the circle would be good.

> The Spirit plays with us [or name of a person in the group]
> The Spirit plays with us
> Dance, sing, let praises ring
> The Spirit plays with us.

Offering: Invite each person to blow a soap bubble as a sign of how we are shaped and loved by God. Be sure to have plenty of soap bubble liquid and blowers!

Joys and Concerns: Invite people to share the good, bad, and blah of their lives either in one big group or in several smaller groups. After collecting the concerns and the joys, pray silently.

Hymn: "Breathe on Me, Breath of God" (in many traditional hymnals).

Benediction: All blow on one another's foreheads, saying, "The Spirit of God be in you."

FRUITS OF THE SPIRIT
(*A Family Liturgy*)

Worship Setting: Your worship setting will depend on which alternative you choose for the sermon. Read through the entire service, make your choices, and then design your setting. Be sure to have enough space for the families to move around and do the activities suggested. Since several of these activities are to be done by families and since not everyone will come in a family group, find some way to help everyone be adopted into a family for this service, which emphasizes that we are all part of the family of God. This can be accomplished with a seating arrangement. If chairs are in groups of six, you can encourage people to join such a group until all seats are occupied. As people arrive, give them a sheet of paper and a crayon and ask them to draw a picture featuring their favorite fruit.

Prelude: Happy music

Call to Worship: Following an informal welcoming by the worship leader, persons will be encouraged to share their pictures of fruit. If the group is large, several subgroups can share. If it is small, ask for volunteers from the total group.

LEADER: We gather to thank God for all the wonderful fruits we have been given.

CONGREGATION: Thank you, God, for [name your favorite fruit.]

LEADER: But we gather also to celebrate a different kind of fruit—the fruits of the Spirit.

CONGREGATION: The fruits we receive from nature help us grow physically and stay healthy.

LEADER: The fruits of the Spirit help us grow in becoming loving persons who share them with others.

CONGREGATION: So let us celebrate these fruits today!

Hymn: "Thank God" (p. 14), or another hymn of thankfulness to God.

A Time of Confession: It has been said that we are often cruelest to those we love the most. All of us have been guilty at times of living the opposite of the fruits of the Spirit. In your family groupings discuss some of the ways in which you have been unloving to one another.

Words of Assurance:

The essence of love is forgiveness. As Christians we have been taught this supremely through Christ's death on the cross. To forgive another is to say, "I love you anyway." Spend a few minutes telling your family that you love them.

Scripture Readings:

Isaiah 35:1–10. You might want to encourage some members of the congregation to dance to this Scripture.

LEFT: The wilderness and the dry land shall be glad,
the desert shall rejoice and bloom,

RIGHT: It shall bloom forth with wild flowers,
with bright jonquils.

LEFT: It shall sing and shout for joy.

RIGHT: The desert will be as glorious as Lebanon,
its splendor like the fertile fields
of Carmel and Sharon.

LEFT: Everyone shall see God's glory,
the splendor of our Creator.

RIGHT: Give strength to tired hands,
steady all trembling knees,

LEFT: Tell those who are downhearted,
"Have courage! Don't be afraid.

RIGHT: God is coming to your rescue
and your enemies will not overtake you."

LEFT: Then the eyes of the blind will see
and the ears of the deaf will hear.

RIGHT: The lame will leap like the deer
and those who can't speak will
sing for joy.

LEFT: Rivers of water will flow through the desert;
The burning sand will become a great lake,

and the dry land will gush forth with water.

RIGHT: Where jackals used to live
will grow reeds and rushes.

LEFT: Through the desert will run a highway,
called "The Road of Holiness,"

RIGHT: And on it shall no sinner walk
nor fools stray along it.

LEFT: No lions shall be there;
no fierce animals roam upon it.

RIGHT: But the redeemed will travel down that way,
those rescued by God shall return on that road.

ALL: They will come to Zion with singing,
and with everlasting joy on their faces:
gladness and joy will go with them,
and they will be forever free from sorrow and grief.[13]

Galatians 5:16–25

Sermon: Below are three sermon ideas. Our hope is that these
will set your mind to working so that you come up with your
own service. Combine some of these ideas, add to them, or
subtract from them. Try to plan the service that will work
best in your situation.

1.   In this service extensive use is made of the song "The
Fruits of the Spirit" found on p. 132. Tom is the writer
and copyright owner of this song, and he is happy to
extend to you the right to reproduce it for use within
your own congregation at no charge. Such reproduction
should include the copyright notation found at the bot-
tom of the song and the words "Used by Permission."
Write to him for permission to reproduce it for other
uses.

One way to use this song is to work with different age
groups ahead of time in children's choirs or in church
school so that they already know the song and will have
learned about the people mentioned in it. Each group
would take a verse and act out part or all of it (you'll need

five groups). This will give the children an opportunity to learn in depth about two biblical characters while at the same time working toward a better understanding of two fruits of the Spirit. These short plays would then be acted out as the sermon for the whole congregation in between the singing of each verse of the song. You may want to have a soloist or a choir sing the verses and ask the whole congregation to join in on the refrain.

2. In this service extensive use is also made of the song, but instead of having children act out the verses, the minister might tell the stories of several of the characters. If the minister is a good storyteller, this can be a fascinating experience for people of all ages.

3. An old tree branch is propped up so that all can see it. On the branch are various intriguing and unusual symbols to represent the "fruits of the Spirit." For example, Tom has used a Snoopy dog to represent joy because of Snoopy's irrepressible spirit, which helps him dance through life no matter what. Gentleness could be a dove, or it might be a baseball bat to represent a fellow you grew up with who coached your grade school team with a spirit of beautiful gentleness. Each symbol will suggest a story, and the telling of them will be your sermon. A variation is to invite ahead of time members of your worship committee or any other interested group, including some children, to put one symbol on the tree for a particular fruit of the Spirit. Each of them would explain the significance of his or her symbol.

Offering: What fruits can you share? We encourage you not only to offer money but also to offer a particular talent, one of the fruits of the Spirit, that you will be working on especially. (The fruits for the love feast should be placed on the table at this time, see love feast section.)

Sharing Joys and Concerns: Do this in whatever way seems most appropriate for your congregation.

A Love Feast—Sharing Fruits: If your budget will allow, have available different kinds of fruits all washed and ready to be eaten. Tables can be stationed around the worship room, and at the time of the offering persons from the congregation who have been asked ahead of time can bring the fruits forward and place them on the tables. The minister will then say:

And now I invite you to come to any of these tables and share in the fruits of God. As you experience their sweet goodness, remember the other fruits of the Spirit that God has provided us and be thankful for both. Share these fruits with one another as an act of love and care. May they nourish you in both body and spirit.

Hymn: "By Their Fruit" (p. 92), or another hymn whose theme is the fruits of the spirit.

Benediction: You are known by your fruits. When people see you, may they see God. Amen.

Postlude: Joyful music

The Fruits of the Spirit

Words and Music by
Thomas Neufer Emswiler

Refrain

Gen - tle - ness, trust - ful - ness, kind - ness, good - ness, pa - tience and

self - con - trol, love, joy, peace:_____ these

are the fruits of the spir - it that make us whole._____

1. The gen-tle-ness of Eve   cra - dl - ing the first hu - man child.
2. The kind-li-ness of Paul   wel - com-ing the gen - tiles to faith.
3. The pa-tience of kind Job   wait - ing to com - pre - hend God's will.
4. The love of Ma - ry Mag-da-lene reach- ing to the cross and be - yond.
5. And peace for all who walk   in the way that Christ has shown us.

The trust-ful-ness of Ruth   choos-ing a new fam-'ly and new God.
The good-ness of Zac - chae - us,   giv - ing back four-fold those he had cheat - ed.
Ho - se - a's self-con - trol,   lov - ing Go - mer when she was un - faith - ful.
The joy-ous-ness of Ma - ry,   bear - ing the Christ glad-ly and with hope.
The peace that pass-es un - der-stand-ing lead - ing to the whole-ness of Sha - lom.

A SERVICE OF BAPTISM, CONFIRMATION, AND RENEWAL*

(This service is designed to be used within a service of congregational worship.)

Introduction: Baptism is the rite of initiation into the church. It is a dramatic way of saying that we accept and affirm God's love for us as we experience a new birth by water and the Spirit. We affirm what we pledged or what was pledged for us in baptism through confirmation, other baptismal renewals, and through the sacrament of Communion.

Presentation of the Candidates: (This may take place at the back of the church, with the candidates knocking on the door seeking admission, or the candidates may come from the congregation to the front of the church.)

LEADER: Behold, these persons [name them] desire to be admitted into the body of Christ through baptism.

OR

I present [names] for confirmation.

OR

I present [names] for the renewal of their baptismal covenant.

How do you respond to these persons?

CONGREGATION: We welcome them into this household of faith with joy and love. As they affirm [or reaffirm] their baptismal vows, we will do the same.

The Expression of Repentance and Commitment:

(If infants are being presented for baptism, the following is included.)

MINISTER: Do you, in presenting this child for baptism, reaffirm your own faith in Christ and the vows made at your baptism?

---

*This service is partly based on *A Service of Baptism, Confirmation, and Renewal,* copyright © 1976 by The United Methodist Church (Nashville, Tenn.: Parthenon Press).

PARENTS: I do.

MINISTER: As parents, you are taking the baptismal vows on behalf of your child. One day this child will be given the opportunity to confirm these vows for him/herself.

(The following vows are addressed to the candidate(s) or, in the case of infant baptism, to the parents.)

MINISTER: Christ calls us to repentance. This means turning around and living a new life. It means turning from sin to righteousness. For the whole church I ask you, do you renounce the captivity of sin and accept the liberty God promises to those who follow God's commandments?

CANDIDATE AND/OR PARENTS: I do.

MINISTER: Do you confess Jesus as the Christ and do you promise to be loyal to the realm the Christ has opened for all people in which no human divisions and distinctions exist and all are one in Christ's love?

CANDIDATE AND/OR PARENTS: I do.

MINISTER: Will you fight the powers of evil in whatever form they present themselves?

CANDIDATE AND/OR PARENTS: I will.

MINISTER: With God's help do you pledge to live a Christian life, be [a] faithful member[s] of Christ's church, and serve as [an] ambassador[s] for God in the world?

CANDIDATE AND/OR PARENTS: I do.

(The following is addressed to the parents of infants.)

MINISTER: As parents, do you accept the responsibility to live before your child a life exemplifying Christ's gospel and to attempt in all ways to teach her/him to follow the Christ so that one day your child can confirm these vows made here by you?

PARENTS: I do.

Thanksgiving over the Water:

LEADER: Creative God: You formed us and this world out of the dark waters of chaos. And time and again you have saved us as we have passed through the waters.

CONGREGATION: We remember the flood and your gracious
promise sealed in the rainbow.   We remember the flight
from Egypt and the way you parted the sea before us.   We
remember Jesus and the way he was protected by the water
of Mary's womb.   We remember John and the way he
baptized Jesus with water.   We remember the disciples
and the way in which they shared in the baptism of Jesus'
death and resurrection and went on to make disciples
throughout the world.

LEADER: And so we come before you today, O God, grateful
for the promise and power of water. We pray that your
Holy Spirit bless this gift of water [pour water into bowl.
If you will be using the pouring method, see complete
discussion of methods to be used on pp. 86–87] and those
who receive it. Wash them in your love and clothe them in
your peace as persons who have died and been raised to
new life with Christ.

The Baptism: As the water is administered, the minister says:
[Name of the candidate], I baptize you in the name of God
the Father/Mother, the Christ, and Holy Spirit. Amen.

OR

I baptize you in the name of God the Creator, Redeemer, and
Sustainer. Amen.

As hands are placed on the heads of those baptized, the
minister says:
God's Holy Spirit is in you. Be faithful to Jesus Christ. Amen.

When all candidates have been baptized, the minister says:
Welcome into the hospitality of God's love as evidenced in
this particular church. We witness with joy your becoming a
part of the Body of Christ.

Confirmation and Other Renewal of Baptism: Water may
be used to trace the cross on the forehead of each person being
confirmed or receiving other baptismal renewal, or water may
be sprinkled toward all persons being confirmed or making

other baptismal renewal while these words are said: [Name of candidate], remember your baptism. Thanks be to God! If sprinkling is used, you may also wish to place hands on the head of each person separately saying to each: [Name of candidate], do not forget that you are a part of the hospitality of God's love. May God's spirit help you to continue to be faithful to Jesus Christ. Amen.

Profession or Renewal of Full Membership in a Particular Church: Follow the form used in your denomination for this commitment.

Welcoming:
  LEADER: Here they are, new colleagues in the faith. Be with them, help them in every way you can, be open to them both in what you can give to them and what they can give to you.
  CONGREGATION: We thank God for these persons and for the faith that is in them.

  We pledge ourselves to work with them to be faithful stewards of God's love in our world. Amen.

AN ORDER FOR THE CELEBRATION OF MARRIAGE

Worship Setting: The setting for this service is a church worship area. It is decorated joyfully and tastefully with flowers
brought by friends of the bride and groom and with banners
made for this occasion by a friend of the couple. With adaptation this service could also be performed in a home, outside,
or in some other setting that has special meaning for the
persons involved. Rather than being separated from the
guests that are arriving and from each other, the groom and
bride are greeting people as they arrive.

Prelude: Joyful music the couple has chosen

Call to Worship: We welcome all of you on this joyful day
as we join together in this worship service celebrating the
marriage of _____ and _____. We invite you to come to this
service not only with joy but also with seriousness as we
affirm and bless the commitment that is being proclaimed
before God and all of us gathered here.

Processional: A joyful hymn is played as the entire wedding
party enters together, and then it is played again as the congregation joins in singing it. The bride and groom process
together at the end of the group.

Words of Welcome from the Bride and Groom: Both bride
and groom tell the congregation how much this service means
to them. If desired, the congregation can at this time greet one
another.

Act of Praise: This is a time reserved for a friend of the groom
or bride to share an artistic expression—music, dance, a light
show, poem, even a short film—of praise to God.

Call to Confession: In the midst of our most hopeful and
joyful times, we remember that we are human beings who
miss the mark of God's high calling time after time. We need
to admit our failures and ask for God's help.

General Prayer of Confession: O God of love, we come to you knowing the goodness of people, the love and care and compassion we sometimes show one another, but don't let us forget our other side. Don't let us forget the pain and heartbreak that are even now a part of our lives and the life of the world as a whole. While we are celebrating this new union, others are enduring the pain of divorce. While we are enjoying wedding feasts and parties, others are starving because of the way in which we humans have divided the world's goods. While we sing and pray to you, God, others have shut themselves off from knowing the transforming power of your love in their lives. Help us, God, to be ever mindful of the needs of this world. Help us to see this union we celebrate today as formed not only to bring greater joy and happiness to the two persons involved, but also as directed outward in concern and care for the aches of the world. In Jesus' name we pray, Amen.

Words of Assurance: God is with us in our struggles to live faithful, loving lives. God does not condemn us when we fail, but rather God is beside us helping us to begin again. No matter what has happened, we can start over.

Scripture Readings:
Psalm 150 (p. 175, no. 5), to be read in joyful unison: Praise God everywhere! Praise God in churches, in heaven and earth, for God's mighty deeds and marvelous greatness! Praise God with trumpets, harps, lyres, drums, dancing, flutes, cymbals, and all things that express joy. Let everything that breathes praise God. *Praise be to God!*[15]

1 Corinthians 13

Sermon: *The Bright Horizons of Love.* The sermon centers on the metaphor of the horizon. You never get to it; it is always beyond. The horizon is a poetic expression of the meaning of love in a relationship such as marriage. In the many and mysterious ways in which Paul described love in 1 Corinthians 13, we never fully know all that love is. Its fullness is always beyond, and of course that is part of what makes marriage or any deep loving relationship a continual adventure.

An Affirmation   (to be proclaimed by everyone):

We believe in love.
We believe in families.
We believe that one of the best structures for love is the
  family.
We believe that family begins
As a man and a woman leave their parents
And forge a new bond together.
We believe that family does not end
Until it encompasses the whole earth.
We believe in love.
We dedicate ourselves to be love's ambassadors for the whole
  world.
Amen.

The Invitation: I now invite the bride and groom and all members of the wedding party to come and stand before me here at the communion table. This is the moment for which we have all been waiting. This is the time when each of us acts as a joyful witness to the commitment _____ and _____ are making to each other. Let us listen in prayerful wonder to this declaration of love. (The bride and groom face each other and say their vows. It is not necessary for the vows to be said from memory. They may be read from small cards if that is more comfortable.)

Exchange of Vows: I choose you above all others to share my life. In doing this I choose to share with you all my times, the bad ones as well as the good. I will cherish you and care for you no matter what happens. I will join with you in directing our lives outward in concern for the whole world family. I make this pledge without time limits and in utter seriousness from this day forward.
  [If rings or other tokens are given:]

And I give you this ring as a sign of what we have pledged here today.

The Announcement: It gives me great pleasure to announce on behalf of all the witnesses gathered here that _____ and _____ are husband and wife according to their own promises given just now and according to the laws of this state. May they find great happiness and deep love as marriage partners.

The Blessing: Traditionally the wedding blessing was given by the families of the couple. They are still an essential part of the blessing, but each of you is joining in blessing this union by your presence here today. We invite you now to express your solid support of this marriage by giving _____ and _____ a standing ovation.

Communion: As the applause continues, a man and a woman from the congregation bring the communion elements forward and place them on the communion table. The minister motions for silence and for the congregation, including the wedding party, to be seated. She or he then lifts the elements and says:

The gifts of God for the people of God.
(The congregation responds with "Amen.")

Communion is always a time for being reminded of promises. In this service we remember our Hebrew heritage and the way in which this supper is patterned after the Passover meal celebrating the ancient Hebrews' liberation from slavery. That meal is a reminder of how God's promise to bring the Hebrew people to a new land was kept, but it is also a reminder of what we as Christians see as the fulfillment of God's promises in Jesus Christ. The covenant God established with the Hebrew people is renewed and deepened in Jesus Christ. It is a covenant of faithfulness sealed in Jesus' blood and reaffirmed in the miracle of the resurrection. It is important to celebrate this supper as we focus on the covenant between _____ and _____. May it help them affirm the possibilities for resurrections in their own relationship, which can help them keep their covenant daily. May it show them and all of us how closely God's love is with us each moment of our lives.

On the same night when Jesus was betrayed, he took bread and broke it [take the loaf and break it], saying, "This is my body broken for you. Eat this in remembrance of me."

Likewise after supper he took the cup [lift the cup] and said, "This cup is the new covenant of my blood shed for you and for many for the forgiveness of sin. Drink this all of you in remembrance of me."

(The whole congregation is invited to take communion at this time in whatever manner seems most appropriate. Music may be played or sung.)

Prayer of Thanksgiving: Words can never fully express what is in our hearts, O God. Our hearts are full now. We are hope-filled. We go forth from this place with new strength and joy. Your meal has helped us to know how much you are with us. Thank you for not giving up on us. Thank you for inspiring people such as _____ and _____ to love each other. Be with them and us all as we leave this place. Amen.

Hymn: "Together" (p. 161), or another special wedding hymn.

Benediction: Go forth bound together by the love of God. Go with hope and joy and with a heart full of dreams, knowing that God is always with you. Amen.

Postlude

A WITNESS TO THE RESURRECTION:
A FUNERAL SERVICE

Prelude: Gentle, quiet music

Call to Worship:
    LEADER: Blessed are those who mourn,
    CONGREGATION: For they shall be comforted.
    LEADER: We come in mourning for someone we love, but we worship in the knowledge that death is not the end. We celebrate the resurrection, the final triumph of God's love, the ultimate hope of every Christian.

Hymn of Praise: Choose a hymn of strength, preferably a favorite of the deceased.

Call to Prayer: Let us pray for faith and understanding in the face of death.

Congregational Prayer: O God, Creator of all life, help us to accept death as a special part of life, trusting in your goodness and great love for every one of us. We feel now the pain of parting with one we love, but we rejoice that we were privileged to experience life with _____. We entrust _____ to you in death, as in life you entrusted him/her to us. We pray in the name of Jesus Christ, through whom you have offered to each of us your great gift of eternal life. Amen.

Scripture Reading: Choose a psalm of God's comfort and love either to read yourself or to read responsively with the congregation. If the deceased had a favorite psalm that is appropriate, it would be good to read it.

Affirmation of Faith:

We believe that God never gives up on us.
We believe that Jesus was God in human form who showed us the astounding steadfastness of God's love for us.
We believe God's Holy Spirit is always with us
even in times of deep suffering and sorrow.

We know that God's love for us continues
>   and continues
>   and continues.
Nothing,
>   not even death,
>   can separate us from this love.[16]

Solo: "Shepherd, Shepherd" (p. 159): as this is sung, encourage people to spend some moments in personal remembrances, reflecting on their relationships with the deceased; or another reflective song about death and our Christian faith.

Scripture Readings:

Isaiah: 43:1–3 (perhaps using this paraphrase by us)
>   But now God says,
>   Who created you, O Jacob, who formed you, O Israel?
>   Fear not, I have redeemed you.
>   I have called you by name and you are mine!
>   When you pass through the waters, I will be with you;
>   When you walk through the fire, you will not be burned,
>   For I am your God.
>   I am your Savior.

Romans 8:31–32, 35, 37–39
LEADER: If God is for us, who can finally be against us?
CONGREGATION: God did not even spare Jesus, but gave him up for us all. Such an act of profound unselfishness is a sign of God's lavish love that provides us with all that we need.
LEADER: Nothing, therefore, can separate us from the love of Christ; not troubles or pain or persecution, not even lack of clothes or food, not even threats of violence or death.
CONGREGATION: For I am absolutely convinced of this: neither death nor life, neither supernatural nor governmental power, nothing that exists and nothing still to come, no power, no height, or depth, or any created thing can ever come between us and the love God made visible in Christ Jesus.[17]

Sermon: *Through Troubled Water.* The sermon will emphasize
God's promise to be with us even in times of great heartache
and trouble such as death. It will focus on the comforting
power of Scripture, referring to the passages used in the
Scripture readings, the passages yet to come in the service, the
resurrection discussion in 1 Corinthians 15, and other appropriate passages. It will also use for inspiration and guidance
the book on death entitled *Through Troubled Water* by William H. Armstrong.[18] The sermon will include a time for
remembering some of the good and beautiful characteristics
and actions of the deceased. This can be shared either by the
minister in charge or by family and friends.

Hymn of Offering: "Jesus, You Are with Us" (p. 88), first
two stanzas, or another communion hymn. As the hymn is
sung, the communion elements are brought forward by members of the congregation and placed on the table.

The Great Thanksgiving:
   LEADER: God who raised up Jesus, will raise us up also by
   God's power (1 Cor. 15:22).
   CONGREGATION: And so we are thankful and comforted, not
   only by remembering and rejoicing in the life of _____
   who has died, but also by knowing the power of God's
   resurrection.
   LEADER: Our eyes have not seen, our ears have not heard; it
   has hardly dawned on us what God has prepared for us (1
   Cor. 2:9).
   CONGREGATION: Our friend has gone before us into the new
   Jerusalem, where there is no more sorrow, no more weeping
   or pain, but only peace and joy with God.
   LEADER: We rejoice for our friend, and we participate with
   her/him through the feast of heaven, this experience of
   Holy Communion. It is in this service that we come to
   know most profoundly the truth of Jesus' death and the
   power of his resurrection.
   CONGREGATION: We are hungry. We need to be fed.

LEADER: (lifting the elements): The gifts of God for the people of God.

CONGREGATION: Amen.

LEADER: Jesus knew he was to face death. He knew the pain and suffering that was before him. He knew too the significance of this for all humanity. And so in the upper room after supper he took bread and broke it and gave it to his disciples saying, "This is my body broken for you. Eat this in remembrance of me." Likewise after supper he took the cup and he said, "This cup is the new covenant in my blood, shed for you and for many for the forgiveness of sin. Drink this all of you in remembrance of me."

The Sharing of Communion: All who wish to partake should be encouraged to do so.

Prayer of Thanksgiving: (in unison)

We have received the bread of life, the cup of salvation. We have received strength and encouragement to continue our daily lives. Help us to remember _____ and be always grateful for the gift of her/his life. Help us to be sensitive and caring to one another as we strive to live on in the spirit and love of the one who always goes before us, Jesus the Christ. Amen.

Hymn: Another song of strength and courage, perhaps a favorite of the deceased.

Benediction: Go, knowing that God goes with you, helping you through the troubled waters of your soul. Go, knowing that nothing, not even death, can defeat God's strong love proclaimed most mightily in the resurrection. Thanks be to God. Amen.

A SERVICE OF HEALING

A service of this nature is best held with only those present who are genuinely concerned about the church's healing ministry. That is, it should not be tacked onto or inserted into a worship service in which many of the participants are skeptical of spiritual healing. It is usually best if those coming know what sort of service they are coming to and are supportive of the healing ministry.

If this is the first time a service of this kind has been held in your congregation, the group will probably be small. We started out meeting in the chapel of a church but soon moved to a carpeted parlor where we could sit in a circle and see one another face to face. This more informal setting has worked better. You may need to experiment to find the best setting for you.

Call to Worship: We gather in the name of the one who was called the Great Physician, the Savior, the one who makes us whole. We gather to offer ourselves as instruments of healing for God's children.

Hymn: "Gifts of Love" (p. 106), or "There Is a Balm in Gilead" (p. 46), or another hymn about healing.

Scripture Reading: One of the healing stories from either the Old or the New Testament. If this is your first service, perhaps several brief healing stories could be read. Allow a few moments for responses, either silent or spoken, to the Scripture readings.

At this point the person leading the service may want to discuss briefly what has been happening in recent years in the area of healing. It should be made clear that no one can promise that a healing will take place. It should also be stated that instantaneous healings are much more the exception than the rule and that people should not be disappointed if no obvious signs of healing are present during the service. That does not mean the healing prayers and service are in vain however. Much healing involves continued prayer over many weeks and months. Even if the body or spirit is not healed immediately, the persons present will have received spiritual food, which is often necessary before any healing can occur in the physical body. Healing often takes time and repeated prayers; don't give up too soon.

A Time of Silent Preparation: Encourage those present to take three or four deep breaths, to relax, and to commune with God in silence, listening to what God may be trying to say to them. This time might be concluded with a short prayer asking God to make the group channels of God's healing power.

Sharing Prayer Concerns: This is the time during which those who seek healing for themselves or for someone else can share their concern. This can be done verbally if the group is small. If the group is large and persons might be inhibited, you might provide small cards on which the names of those in need of healing prayer can be written. These names could then be collected and read aloud. (Some healers feel it is important that the congregation or group not know what the ailments are as they will focus their attention on the illness rather than visualizing the ill person as whole; others do not stress this point. They instead emphasize imagining the destruction or elimination of the illness or pain. Both methods seem to work.)

Intercessory Prayer: In our services, after the names of persons have been shared, we ask those present to relax, close their eyes, and try to imagine the person whole. They may picture the Christ laying hands on the person or see the person surrounded by a white light or simply see the person smiling and happy. It is not necessary to know what the person looks like to do this. They can just imagine what he or she might look like.

If many names have been shared, it is often helpful for the leader slowly to repeat the names of those who are absent, allowing time in between for the visualization prayer. When all the names have been repeated, the leader may want to offer a verbal prayer for God's healing power to come into the lives of those named.

Laying on of Hands: If some of the persons present have requested healing prayers for themselves, this is the time to do that. Ask them to come forward one at a time and sit in a chair you have provided. (If your group is small, you may want to make a circle around the chair or simply have everyone sit on the floor, with the person seeking healing in the middle.) It is important for everyone, especially the one in need of healing, to be relaxed and at ease.

The leader then lays hands on the person, generally on the head or the shoulders, although you may lay hands on the afflicted spot if appropriate. Suggest that the person relax and feel God's healing energy flowing into him or her. In a small group you may all want to join in laying hands on the person. During the laying on of hands it is not necessary to pray verbally; the most important thing is to relax and imagine yourself as a channel for God. Don't concentrate too hard; just let God's healing energy flow through you. You may want to conclude with a brief prayer or blessing for the person and then let the next person come forward.

Benediction: Join hands (in a circle if possible). Encourage each person to be aware of the energy flowing around the room, through them to the others and from the others to them.

Go forth in peace to be agents of healing in a broken world. Amen.

GUIDED IMAGERY MEDITATIONS

The first three of the following guided imagery meditations are suitable for use as part of a sermon; the last one is most appropriate for an evening service or devotion. In preparation for such an experience, the congregation should understand that their participation is voluntary and that the directions are merely suggestions. If they find other images coming to mind, that's all right. They shouldn't be concerned about doing it "right"; however they do it is right for them. They are free to bring into their scene any assistance in the form of other persons or objects. They probably won't be able to imagine the scene as clearly as they can watch a movie; but they should not be concerned about that. If there are interruptions, ask them to acknowledge them and come back to the meditation. You may want to warn them that some people, when getting relaxed for meditations such as these, may fall asleep. That is okay, and they should not be embarrassed by it.

The participants should put everything out of their hands, put their feet flat on the floor, and sit as straight as possible and still be comfortable. (If small children who are too young to participate and need a watchful eye are present, you may want to suggest that one of the parents participate now and perhaps one try it later. Otherwise, neither of them may feel that they can shut their eyes and relax.)

It is important for the participants to take three or four deep breaths, close their eyes, and relax. Allow enough time for this at the beginning of the meditation.

The leader should have rehearsed the meditation enough to be familiar with it. The meditation should be read slowly, with pauses at the appropriate places for the participants to picture the events as suggested.

Following the meditation, allow some time for personal reflection on what has just happened, perhaps even encouraging people to write down some of their thoughts, and for sharing with one another in groups of three or four.

BIRTH

Read Genesis 18:1–15; 21:1–7 and discuss briefly.

Relax, close your eyes, and take three or four deep breaths.

Imagine now that you are Sarah, the old woman. Feel the years within your body. The years have been long and many with your husband, Abraham. Together you and he have traveled across the land in search of a new home, a new life. Together you've tried to be faithful to Yahweh who has promised that you, Sarah, will be the mother of nations. But the years have passed and there has been no child; now you are past the age of childbearing.

You and Abraham are sitting in your tent. Look around you at the tent and out the door to the countryside. What do you see? Suddenly you are aware that three men have appeared outside your tent, and Abraham runs out to greet them. Preparations are made to feed them, and while Abraham is serving them under the tree, you listen to them speaking. You hear one of them ask about you and even call you by name. Now the stranger tells Abraham that at this same time next year, you will have a son.

Let these words sink into you. Now you begin to laugh. How can that be? What thoughts go through your mind as you reflect on these words from the stranger?

Time passes, and you discover that, as crazy as it sounded at the time, what the stranger said has come true: You did become pregnant and have now given birth to a son. Once more you laugh, but this time it is not the laughter of disbelief but the laughter of joy. God has called forth new life from your barren womb.

Now in the quiet, return to the twentieth century to your own body and self. Does a Sarah live within you? Does a part of you, perhaps, disbelieve God's promises, laugh at them? If so, what are some of those promises that you don't believe? Talk with that Sarah part of yourself for awhile.

Does a part of you believe that you are too old to give birth to something new in your life? Does a part of you laugh at you for your hopes and dreams, saying that you are beyond the age of birthing? Talk with her awhile.

Does a part of you laugh with joy at the new life God has called forth from you? What does she laugh over?

When ready, say good-bye to the Sarah within, open your eyes, and return to the group.

HEALING

Read Mark 2:1–12 and discuss briefly.

Relax, close your eyes, and take three or four deep breaths.

It's a beautiful summer day. The sky is blue with a few white puffy clouds floating in it. Picture yourself now in a grassy area where you're relaxing and enjoying yourself. As you rest there, you reflect upon yourself and some part of you that is in need of healing. It may be a part of your body that is not functioning correctly, or perhaps some emotions or some other part of you that needs to be healed. Focus on that part of you.

Now you are joined by four other people who care about you and want you to be whole. Who are those four people? Look at them. Observe their expressions; hear what they say.

The four people now take you in some manner to the Christ. A large crowd is gathered around, but your friends are able to take you right to where the Christ is standing. Get a sense now of yourself there with the Christ. What is said to you? Done to you? Picture yourself now actually being healed of your afflic-tion. If it's a physical ailment, feel the healing energy flowing to that part of your body. If it's an emotional or spiritual heal-ing, find a way to symbolize that healing or listen to hear some special words of guidance from the Christ.

You offer the Christ your thanks, and then you and your four friends leave, rejoicing in your wholeness.

When you are ready, take a deep breath, stretch, open your eyes, and return to the group.

HIDDEN TREASURE

Read Matthew 13:44 and discuss briefly.

Relax, close your eyes, and take three or four deep breaths.

Picture yourself at the edge of a forest. It's a nice summer day, and you decide to walk into the forest. Get a sense of the trees around you, the ground underfoot, the coolness of the forest, the smell of the air, the sounds your feet make as you walk.

As you walk deeper into the forest, you notice something sticking partly out of the ground. You walk over to it and begin to dig it up. Bring into the scene whatever equipment you need to dig up this object. Once it is uncovered, you see that it is something extremely valuable, a real treasure.

Examine this treasure closely. What is it? Does it have any relevance to your life? What other treasures do you have in your life? Are there any you prize above all others? How do you express your joy over the treasures in your life?

The treasure you have found is yours to keep. Do with it what you will and then begin to find your way back out of the forest.

When you're ready to rejoin the group, take a deep breath and open your eyes.

REST

Read Matthew 11:28–30 and discuss briefly.

Relax, close your eyes, take three or four deep breaths.

Think back over your day. Think of the many things you have done. Do some loose ends still call for your attention? Are you ashamed, unhappy, or worried about some events of the day? Reflect on those for a few minutes.

Now imagine that the Christ is standing here in this room holding a large basket. The Christ comes over to you and invites you to place all your worries, all your labors, into that basket. You gather them up and place them inside. Now the Christ lays a hand on your head and gives you a blessing. Slowly you feel the effects of that blessing flowing down over your entire body. You are at rest. Amen.

Appendix

Guidelines for Nonsexist Use of Language*

GENERAL PROBLEMS

Omission of Women

1. Although *man* in its original sense carried the dual meaning of adult human and adult male, its meaning has come to be so closely identified with adult male that the generic use of *man* and other words with masculine markers should be avoided whenever possible.

Examples	*Alternatives*
mankind	humanity, human beings, people
man's achievements	human achievements
the best man for the job	the best person for the job, the best man or woman for the job
man-made	synthetic, manufactured, crafted, machine-made
the common man	the average person, ordinary people

2. The use of *man* in occupational terms when persons holding the jobs could be either female or male should be avoided. English is such a rich language that alternatives to the much maligned — person (as in *congressperson*) can almost always be found (*representative*).

---

*These guidelines are excerpted from the *Guidelines for Nonsexist Use of Language,* copyright © 1976 by the National Council of Teachers of English. Reprinted by permission of the publisher and the author.

Examples	*Alternatives*
chairman	coordinator (of a committee or department), moderator (of a meeting), presiding officer, head, chair
businessman, fireman, mailman	business executive or manager, fire fighter, mail carrier

In the interest of parallel treatment, job titles for women and men should be the same.

Examples	*Alternatives*
steward and stewardess	flight attendant
policeman and policewoman	police officer

3. Because English has no generic singular — or common-sex — pronoun, we have used *he, his,* and *him* in such expressions as "the student . . . he." When we constantly personify "the judge," "the critic," "the executive," "the author," etc., as male by using the pronoun *he,* we are subtly conditioning ourselves against the idea of a female judge, critic, executive, or author. There are several alternative approaches for ending the exclusion of women that results from the pervasive use of the masculine pronouns.

a. Recast into the plural.

Example	*Alternative*
Give each student his paper as soon as he is finished.	Give students their papers as soon as they are finished.

b. Reword to eliminate unnecessary gender problems.

Example	*Alternative*
The average student is worried about his grades.	The average student is worried about grades.

c. Replace the masculine pronoun with *one, you,* or (sparingly) *he or she,* as appropriate.

Example	*Alternative*
If the student was satisfied with his performance on the pretest, he took the posttest.	A student who was satisfied with her or his performance on the pretest took the posttest.

d. Alternate male and female examples and expressions.

Examples	*Alternative*
Let each student participate.	Let each student participate.
Has he had a chance to talk?	Has she had a chance to talk?
Could he feel left out?	Could he feel left out?

4. Using the masculine pronouns to refer to an indefinite pronoun (*everybody, everyone, anybody, anyone*) also has the effect of excluding women. In all but strictly formal usage, plural pronouns have become acceptable substitutes for the masculine singular.

Example	*Alternative*
Anyone who wants to go to the game should bring his money tomorrow.	Anyone who wants to go to the game should bring their money tomorrow.

5. Certain phrases inadvertently exclude women by assuming that all readers are men.

Example	*Alternative*
NOTE convention-goers and their wives are invited . . .	NOTE convention-goers and their spouses are invited . . .

Demeaning Women

1. Men and women should be treated in a parallel manner, whether the description involves jobs, appearance, marital status, or titles.

Examples	*Alternatives*
lady lawer	lawyer
Running for Student Council president are Bill Smith, a straight-A sophomore, and Kathie Ryan, a pert junior.	Running for Student Council president are Bill Smith, a straight-A sophomore, and newspaper editor Kathie Ryan, a junior.
Senator Percy and Mrs. Chisholm	Charles Percy and Shirley Chisholm or Mr. Percy and Mrs. Chisholm or Senator Percy and Representative Chisholm

2. Terms or adjectives which patronize or trivialize women or girls should be avoided, as should sexist suffixes and adjectives dependent on stereotyped masculine or feminine markers.

Examples	*Alternatives*
gal Friday	assistant
I'll have my girl do it.	I'll have my secretary do it.
career girl	professional woman, name the woman's profession, e.g., attorney Ellen Smith
ladies	women (unless used with gentlemen)
libber	feminist
coed	student
authoress, poetess	author, poet
man-sized job	big or enormous job
old wives' tale	superstitious belief, story, or idea

Sex-Role Stereotyping

1. Women should be shown as participating equally with men; they should not be omitted or treated as subordinate to men. Thus generic terms such and doctor or nurse should be assumed to include both men and women; "male nurse" and "woman doctor" should be avoided.

Examples	*Alternatives*
Writers become so involved in their work that they neglect their wives and children.	Writers become so involved in their work that they neglect their families.
Sally's husband lets her teach part-time.	Sally teaches part-time.

2. Jobs, roles, or personal characteristics should not be stereotyped by sex.

Examples	*Alternatives*
the elementary teacher . . . she	elementary teachers . . . they
the principal . . . he	principals . . . they
Have your Mother send cookies for the field trip.	Have your parents send cookies for the field trip.

Examples

Write a paragraph about what you expect to do when you are old enough to have Mr. and Mrs. before your name. (spelling exercise)

While lunch was *delayed*, the ladies chattered about last night's meeting.

Alternatives

Write a paragraph about what you expect to do when you grow up.

While lunch was *delayed*, the women talked about last night's meeting.

Sample Revised Passages

Many of the general problems just discussed overlap in practice. Substantial revisions are sometimes necessary:

Example

O'Connors to Head PTA

Jackson High School PTA members elected officers for the 1975-76 school year Wednesday night at the school cafeteria.

Dr. and Mrs. James O'Connor were elected co-presidents from a slate of three couples. Dr. O'Connor, a neurosurgeon on the staff of Howard Hospital, has served for two years on the PTA Budget and Finance Committee. Mrs. O'Connor has been active on the Health and Safety Committee.

Elected as co-vice-presidents were Mr. and Mrs. Tom Severns; secretary, Mrs. John Travers; and treasurer, Mrs. Edward Johnson. Committee chairmen were also selected. Each chairman will be briefed on his responsibilities at a spe-

Alternative

O'Connors to Head PTA

Jackson High School PTA members elected officers for the 1975-76 school year Wednesday night at the school cafeteria.

James and Marilyn O'Connor were elected co-presidents from a slate of three couples. James O'Connor, a neurosurgeon on the staff of Howard Hospital, has served for two years on the PTA Budget and Finance Committee, and Marilyn O'Connor, president of the League of Women Voters, has been active on the PTA Health and Safety Committee for three years.

Elected as co-vice-presidents were Jane and Tom Severns; secretary, Ann Travers; and treasurer, Susan Johnson. Committee coordinators

cial meeting on June 3. The revised budget will be presented at that meeting.

Principal Dick Wade announced that Mrs. Elizabeth Sullivan had been chosen Teacher of the Year by the Junior Women's League. She was nominated in a letter written by ten of her students. Each student discussed how she had influenced him.

Mrs. Sullivan, an English teacher at Jackson for ten years, is the wife of Joseph Sullivan, a partner in the law firm of Parker, Sullivan and Jordon, and the mother of two Jackson students.

Smartly attired in a blue tweed suit, Mrs. Sullivan briefly addressed the group, expressing her gratitude at receiving the award.

were also selected and will be briefed on their responsibilities at a special meeting on June 3. The revised budget will be presented at that meeting.

Dick Wade, principal of Jackson High School, announced that Elizabeth Sullivan, an English teacher at Jackson for ten years, had been chosen Teacher of the Year by the Junior Women's League. She was nominated in a letter written by ten of her students. Each of the students, discussed how they had been influenced by her.

Sullivan briefly addressed the group, expressing her pleasure at receiving the award.

Guidelines for Nonsexist Use of Language about God*

GENERAL PROBLEMS

Omission of Feminine References to God

1. Although theologians are almost unanimous in asserting that God includes and/or goes beyond all sexual categories, most theologians and other folks referring to God still use masculine words exclusively. This shows up in two ways:
    A. Through the use of masculine titles for God
    Examples: Lord, King, Father, Master

---

*Reprinted from *Put on Your Party Clothes,* edited by Sharon and Tom Neufer Emswiler (Normal, Ill.: The Wesley Foundation, 1977). Used by permission.

Alternatives: Ruler, Sovereign, Creator, Parent

(Note—a second alternative is to balance masculine references for God with feminine ones. This works well with Father/Mother, and fairly well with King/Queen, but because of accumulated cultural meanings fairly well breaks down with Lord/Lady and certainly with Master/Mistress.

B. Through the English pronoun problem. Since English has no common gender pronoun, "he" has almost always been used in referring to God.

Examples: God loves you. He cares for you. He will be with you always.

Alternatives: God loves you. God cares for you. *Yahweh* will be with you always.

(Note—other alternatives to repeating the word God or using the Hebrew *Yahweh* include the following: recasting the sentence—God loves you, cares for you, and will be with you always.; balancing pronouns—God loves you. He cares for you. She will be with you always.; using "it"—God loves you. It cares for you. It will be with you always. Although this last alternative seems especially repugnant to most folks who treasure belief in a personal God, perhaps the problem lies not with the word "it," but with our conception of objects. Can an "it" be a "thou?") The same solutions are also possible for other forms of the pronoun.

Example: God himself cares for you.

Alternatives: God Godself cares for you. God himself/herself cares for you. God cares for you.

2. Not only is the word God identified with the masculine, but so is the entire Trinity. This can be pin-pointed in the following ways:

A. The Trinitarian formula—although the history of this formula is of vital importance and its significance as an ecumenical unifying point should not be underrated, we believe it is inexcusable to use this traditional formula all or even most of the time.

Examples: Father, Son and Holy Spirit.

Alternatives: God, Jesus (or the Christ or Jesus Christ),

and Holy Spirit, Creator, Redeemer, Sustainer. Creator, Liberator, Advocate.

B. The important thing about affirmations concerning Jesus as a "man" is not that he became male but that he became human.
   Examples: Jesus, the man ... Son of Man.
   Alternatives: Jesus, the person ... Child of Humanity. Humanity's Child.

C. The word for Holy Spirit in Hebrew is feminine and in Greek is neuter, thus translations could use at least the pronoun "it" if not "she" when referring to the Holy Spirit.
   Examples: The Holy Spirit ... he will come.
   Alternatives: The Holy Spirit ... it will come. The Holy Spirit ... she will come. The Holy Spirit will come.

Other Concerns Relating to God-Language

1. Try to discover as many nonsexual images for God as you can. They abound both in the Bible and in contemporary literature.
   Examples: Light, Rock, Glory, Truth, Love, Ground of Being, Fire, First and Last.

2. To help people be more aware of the analogical character of all our language for God it is helpful to restructure prayers and other liturgical formulations as similes rather than as metaphors.
   Examples: O Father, we pray for your help ... O Mother, we pray for your presence ...
   Alternatives: O God, who watches over us like a father, we pray for your help ... O God, who cares for us like a mother hovering over her young, we pray for your presence ...

3. If you do use sexual images for God, it is good to try to find some that go beyond our sexual stereotypes.
   Examples: God as strong father or nurturing mother.
   Alternatives: God as a woman searching for her coin or a man painting a beautiful picture.

4. Alternatives need to be found for other descriptions of God's presence.
   Example: Kingdom of God.
   Alternatives: Realm of God. Reign of God. Rule of God. The Age to Come.

Films for Use in Worship

What follows is only a small selection of what is available for use in worship. We have suggested some specific ways each film may be used, but don't feel limited to these suggestions. You know your own setting and needs best. The initials after each film indicate at least one source where it may be obtained. The complete address is listed at the end of this section.

The Dancing Prophet (Franciscan Communications Center, 15 minutes). This is the story of the black dancer Doug Crutchfield, his work with crippled and elderly people in Denmark, and his dramatic dances of faith in worship. It is also the story of the conflict between Doug and his father, a minister in the United States who is suspicious of dance in the church but who finally affirms Doug's ministry, and of Doug's feelings of being rejected by a racist society in the United States. It makes a powerful sermon on the theme of accepting one another, dancing our faith, or using our gifts. Needs some interpretation with the average congregation. UMFS.

A Day in the Life of Bonnie Consolo (Barr, 21 minutes). This is the inspiring story of Bonnie Consolo, a person born without arms, and how she has managed to cope marvelously with this handicap. It can be the major part of a sermon on blooming where you are planted or a beautiful act of dedication as people are encouraged to see all the possibilities they have before them when compared to Bonnie and what she can do. UMFS.

Faith (Ikonographics, 1 min.) In human, everyday terms this film places us in touch with the wonder and mystery of the faith experience. Makes a striking Affirmation of Faith. IK

A Fuzzy Tale (UMC, 12 minutes). This is a happy parable about caring and not being afraid to show it! Based on Carl Steiner's well-known story, *A Fuzzy Tale* helps us experience how easily gossip combined with greed and envy can create cold loneliness. When a small child has the courage to question "the way things have become," warm fuzzies begin flowing again. Excellent for a sermon on caring or on the power of the tongue as described in the Book of James. MM

He Leadeth Me (Gospel, 30 minutes). This is a brief film biography of Ken Medema, a dynamic young singer-pianist-composer. He is the director of music and creative art therapies at the Essex County New

Jersey Psychiatric Hospital. He also happens to be blind. He is a joyful, creative, real human being who refuses to accept blindness as any more of a handicap than other people have. Could be used as a sermon about the meaning of handicaps or the power of music to express our faith. G.

Included Out (Sharon Neufer Emswiler, 2 minutes). This is a humorous parable about the way in which sexist language in worship excludes at least half the congregation. A woman from another culture is attempting to understand how English is used in a typical worship service. Just when she thinks she knows all about "generic" usage, she discovers that it isn't all that simple. This can be an excellent introduction to a sermon dealing with sexist language concerns. MM.

Joseph Schultz (Wombat, 13 minutes). This is a powerful film about individual integrity in the face of group pressure. It is all the more startling because it is based on a true event during World War II. Joseph Schultz is a German soldier fighting in Yugoslavia. He and his comrades are commanded to serve as a firing squad to execute a group of peasants. Schultz refuses and is ordered by his captain to obey orders or join the peasants. Schultz joins the peasants and is killed. The sensitive use of actual photographs helps to add realism to the story. This film is a beautiful expression of Romans 12:1–2. W.

Joy (Ikonographics, 1 minute). Here is a poetic expression of the meaning of real joy as a deep down basic experience of life. It could be used as a Call to Worship or an Act of Praise in a service dealing with joy. Because it is short, you might want to use it twice, near the beginning and at the end of a service. You might want to show the film once without sound and ask people to make up their own narration. Later it could be shown with the sound track. IK.

The Mark of the Clown (Faith and Fantasy, Inc., 15 minutes). This totally nonverbal film shows how a clown transforms an "ordinary" Protestant worship service into a grand celebration. The symbolic actions employed by the clown, especially in relationship to the sacraments and to confession, are extraordinarily powerful. This film could be used as a sermon, or it could be used with your worship committee to help them see the possibilities for developing their own worship services with clowns. MM.

Minnie Remembers (UMC, 5 minutes). This is a touching poem-prayer by an old woman who has been abandoned in her last years. It calls us to be more loving and spontaneous with one another. It is an especially powerful statement on the need for touch all through our lives. Can be part of a sermon dealing with touch as the language of love or a service dealing with aging. MM.

Nail (Family Films, 20 minutes). This film parable is a significant statement of our need for love. It is the whimsical tale of a woman who finds a nail and accidentally discovers how it can serve as a catalyst for bringing together lonely, needy people. The film can be part of a sermon on the need for and meaning of community. It can also be an excellent statement on the nature of worship. UMFS.

Peege (Phoenix Films, 28 minutes). This is the most touching film we have ever used in worship. It is the story of a family's Christmas visit to the father's mother who is in a retirement home. It shows their struggling attempts to communicate with this old and sick woman. It shows finally how one son uses shared memory as a means of reaching his grandmother. It can be the sermon on a day you want to share about communicating memory or about aging. PH.

Present Moment (Ikonographics, 1 minute). This film shows that each moment is precious and important. It helps us see that the way we live each moment is what we make of our life. It can be used as a Call to Prayer or as the Pastoral Prayer. IK.

Sleepy World (Franciscan Communications Center, 1 minute). Shows a little child waking up grumpy parents and telling them he only wanted to give them a kiss. The narrator then reminds us that Jesus came to bestow a kiss on the world. Excellent Call to Worship. TE.

They Shall See (Franciscan Communications Center, 5 minutes). A beautiful, poetic statement through nature photography and instrumental music of the filmmaker's understanding of the beautitude "Blessed are the pure in heart, for they shall see God." Beautiful Call to Worship, Act of Praise, part of a Scripture reading, or part of a sermon. TE.

The Velveteen Rabbit (LBS Productions, 19 minutes). This sensitive live-action film is true to the classic story by Margery Williams. It is a story about the meaning of friendship and love and how someone can be transformed by this love. An excellent sermon film, which would be especially appropriate for family worship. LSB.

The Vision (Sharon and Tom Neufer Emswiler, 2 minutes). This film helps people see the need for expanding our images of God. A man, who thinks he has God wrapped up in a neat box, begins talking with a woman who sees God quite differently. The woman has just had a vision of God, which images God through many different symbols from many different religions and cultures. The film ends in a joke that also raises some serious questions. The film would make an excellent introduction to a sermon dealing with expanding our images of God. MM.

Where Films May Be Obtained

Rental rates vary. Be sure to check free sources such as your denomination's audiovisual library and your public library before renting these films. All these sources have excellent free catalogs. Those marked with an asterisk are especially helpful.

B Stephen Bosustow Productions, P.O. Box 2127, Santa Monica, CA 90406.

G Go.pel Films, Inc., Box 455, Muskegon, MI 49443

*IK Ikonographics, P.O. Box 4454, Louisville, KY 40204

LSB LSB Productions, Educational Films, 1310 Monaco Dr., Pacific Palisades, CA 90272

*MM Mass Media Ministries, 2116 N. Charles St., Baltimore, MD 21218

PH Phoenix Films, 470 Park Av., S., New York, NY 10016

*TE TeleKETICS, Franciscan Communications Center, 1229 S. Santee St., Los Angeles, CA 90015

UMFS United Methodist Film Service, 1525 McGavock St., Nashville, TN 37203

W Wombat Productions, Inc., 77 Tarrytown Road, White Plains, NY 10607

A newsletter that is especially helpful to keep current on films is *Mass Media Newsletter,* published twice monthly, $10 per year from Mass Media Ministries, 2116 N. Charles St., Baltimore, MD 21218.

Notes

Introduction

1. (Wilmington, N.C.: Consortium Press, 1976), pp. ii, iii.
2. (New York: Harper & Row, 1974).
3. (Normal, Ill.: The Wesley Foundation, 1977).

Chapter 1

1. *Hal* meaning whole, sound, happy, as in "hale and hearty."
2. For a beginning study of these concepts, see Hugh C. White, *Shalom in the Old Testament* (Philadelphia: United Church Press, 1973), and Paul L. Hammer, *Shalom in the New Testament* (Philadelphia: United Church Press, 1973).
3. (Geneva, Switzerland: World Council of Churches, 1967), p. 14.
4. *Catholic World,* January 1971.
5. For a good basic description of feminist theology, see Letty M. Russell, *Human Liberation in a Feminist Perspective—A Theology* (Philadelphia: Westminster Press, 1974).
6. See June Singer, *Androgyny: Toward a New Theory of Sexuality* (New York: Anchor Books, 1977).
7. See Audrey Sorrento, ed., *Women Exploring Theology* (Loveland, Ohio: Grailville, 1973).
8. See the research by Sister Justa Smith as reported in Robert Keck, *The Spirit of Synergy* (Nashville: Abingdon, 1978), p. 32.
9. For more information contact the American Holistic Medical Association, Route 2, Welsh Coulee, La Crosse, WI 54601.
10. See "The Good News about Cancer," *New Age* (May 1978), pp. 32 ff.
11. See Francis MacNutt, *The Power to Heal* (Notre Dame, Ind.: Ave Maria Press, 1977).

Chapter 2

1. John Godwin, *Occult America* (New York: Doubleday, 1972), p. 23.
2. (Niles, Ill.: Argus Communications, 1976).

Chapter 3

1. David Randolph, *God's Party: A Guide to New Forms of Worship* (Nashville: Abingdon, 1975), p. 80.
2. Available from Ruth Hoppin, 25 Portola Ave., Daly City, CA 94015.
3. See examples in Tom Neufer Emswiler and Sharon Neufer Emswiler, eds., *Sisters and Brothers, Sing!,* 2d ed. (Normal, Ill.: The Wesley Foundation, 1977).
4. See an attempt at this in Joann Haugerud, *The Word for Us* (Seattle: Coalition on Women and Religion, 1977).

5. See especially Alleen Pace Nilsen, Haig Bosmajiano, H. Lee Gershuny, and Julia P. Stanley, *Sexism and Language* (Urbana, Ill.: National Council of Teachers of English, 1977); Nancy Henley and Barrie Thorne, eds., *Language and Sex: Difference and Dominance* (Rowley, Mass.: Newbury House Publishing, 1975); Barbara Westbrook Eakins and R. Gene Eakins, *Sex Differences in Human Communication* (Boston: Houghton Mifflin, 1978).

6. See V. Kidd, "A Study of the Images Produced through the Use of the Male Pronoun As the Generic," *Moments in Contemporary Rhetoric and Communication* 1 (1971): 25–29.

7. See J. Schneider and S. Hacker, "Sex Role Imagery and Use of the Generic 'Man' in Introductory Texts: A Case in the Sociology of Sociology," *American Sociologist* 8 (1973): 12–18.

8. See S. L. Bem and D. J. Bem, "Does Sex-Biased Job Advertising 'Aid and Abet' Sex Discrimination?" *Journal of Applied Social Psychology* 3 (1973): 6–18.

9. (Urbana, Ill.: National Council of Teachers of English, 1977).

10. Julia P. Stanley, "Gender-Marking in American English," Ibid., pp. 51–52.

11. *Getting Well Again* (Los Angeles: J. P. Tarcher, 1978).

12. Eric Marshall and Stuart Hemple, comps. (New York: Pocket Books, 1966).

13. Feminine references for God include the following: God as mother (Isa. 42:14); as mother hen (Matt. 23:37); as a woman searching for her coin (Luke 15). See also Letty M. Russell, *Human Liberation in a Feminist Perspective—A Theology* (Philadelphia, Westminster Press, 1974), pp. 97–103; and Sharon Neufer Emswiler and Tom Neufer Emswiler, *Women and Worship* (New York: Harper & Row, 1974), pp. 19–25.

14. Distributed by Mass Media Ministries, 2116 North Charles Street, Baltimore, MD 21218.

15. See Letty M. Russell, ed., *The Liberating Word* (Philadelphia: Westminster Press, 1976), pp. 82 ff.

16. (Berkeley, Cal.: Living Love Center, 1972), p. 11.

17. (Chicago: Ecumenical Women's Center, 1974).

Chapter 4

1. Available from David Holmes, 402 South Carroll, Rock Rapids, Iowa 51246.

2. For children's liturgy books that take this approach, see especially W. Thomas Fancher and Ione C. Nieland, *Touching God* (Notre Dame, Ind.: Ave Maria Press, 1975); and Kathleen Sladens, *Let Them Worship* (Toronto: H. S. Publications, 1976). See also Virginia Sloyan and Gabe Huck, eds., *Children's Liturgies* (Washington, D.C.: The Liturgical Conference, 1970); and Virginia Sloyan, ed., *Signs, Songs and Stories—Another Look at Children's Liturgies* (Washington, D.C.: The Liturgical Conference, 1974).

3. A fine annotated list of children's books that can be used in worship is found in Fred Thompson, *Celebrations for Children* (West Mystic, Conn.: Twenty-Third Publications, 1978), pp. 40–52. This list includes summaries of each book, along with suggestions on how it might be used in worship.

4. A helpful book in this area is Kathryn Wright, *Let the Children Sing* (New York: Seabury Press, 1975).

5. For an excellent in-depth look at worship in black churches, see *This Far by Faith* (Washington, D.C.: The National Liturgical Conference, 1977).

6. *The Interpreter,* June 1976.

Chapter 5

1. Two indispensable books in this area are Francis MacNutt, *The Power to Heal* (Notre Dame, Ind.: Ave Maria Press, 1977), and Dennis Linn and Matthew Linn, *Healing Life's Hurts* (New York: Paulist Press, 1977).
2. Carolyn Stahl, *Opening to God* (Nashville: The Upper Room, 1977), pp. 16–17.

Chapter 6

1. See Hans Bernhard Meyer, "The Social Significance of the Liturgy," in *Politics and Liturgy,* ed. Herman Schmidt and David Power (New York: Herder and Herder, 1974), p. 41.
2. See J. G. Davies, *Worship and Mission* (New York: Association Press, 1967) for a full explanation of this theme.
3. Ibid., pp. 135 ff.

Chapter 7

1. Story related in Madeleine L'Engle, *A Circle of Quiet* (New York: Farrar Strauss & Giroux, 1972), p. 172.
2. Ibid., pp. 123–24.
3. Available from TeleKETICS, Franciscan Communications Center, 1229 South Santee Street, Los Angeles, CA 90015.
4. Quoted in Richard Schickel, "Marshall McLuhan: Canada's Intellectual Comet," *Harper's,* November 1965, pp. 62–68.
5. See Doug Adams, *Congregational Dancing in Christian Worship,* rev. ed. (Austin: The Sharing Co., 1971) for a discussion of the history of dance in the church.
6. See Carla De Sola, *The Spirit Moves: A Handbook of Dance and Prayer* (Washington, D.C.: The Liturgical Conference, 1977). See also Sister Adelaide Ortegel, S.P., *A Dancing People* (West Lafayette, Ind.: The Center for Contemporary Celebration, 1976).
7. This concept is beautifully explicated in Garardus Van der Leeuw, *Sacred and Profane Beauty* (New York: Holt, Rinehart, and Winston, 1963).
8. The adaptation by William Prenevost of this story that we used was published in 1979. Available from Contemporary Drama Service, Box 457-GL, Downers Grove, IL 60515, catalog no. 27.
9. This title was inspired in part by *Adam Among the Television Trees: An Anthology of Verse by Contemporary Christian Poets,* ed. Virginia Mollenkott (Waco, Tex.: Word, 1971).
10. Van der Leeuw, *Sacred and Profane Beauty,* p. 215.
11. For an excellent discussion of this, see Kent Schneider, *The Creative Musician in the Church* (West Lafayette, Ind.: The Center for Contemporary Celebration, 1976), pp. 12 ff.
12. For some examples of secular songs that can be used in worship, see Carlton Young, *Exodus* (Carol Stream, Ill.: Agape, 1976).
13. See H. Grady Hardin, Joseph D. Quillion, and James F. White, *The Celebration of the Gospel—A Study in Christian Worship* (Nashville: Abingdon, 1964), especially pp. 153 ff.
14. For more information on this topic, see James F. White, *Protestant Worship and Church Architecture* (New York: Oxford University Press, 1964).
15. Hardin, Quillion, and White, *The Celebration of the Gospel,* pp. 157 ff.

Chapter 8

1. For an interesting attempt to do this in six specific services, see Edwin R. Lincoln, *The Senses and the Soul—Introducing the Eccentric into Worship* (Lima, Ohio: C. S. S. Publishing Co., 1975).
2. For interesting discussions in this field, see Ruth Winter, *The Smell Book: Scents, Sex, and Society* (Philadelphia: J. B. Lippincott, 1976)—see especially p. 22 for a report of a study showing the relationship of smell to memory; and George D. Armerding, *The Fragrance of the Lord* (San Francisco: Harper & Row, 1979).

Chapter 9

1. Geddes MacGregor, *The Rhythm of God—A Philosophy of Worship* (New York: Seabury Press, 1974), p. 15.
2. Ibid., pp. 10 ff.
3. Ibid., p. 37.

Chapter 10

1. Geddes MacGregor, *The Rhythm of God—A Philosophy of Worship* (New York: Seabury Press, 1974), p. 8.
2. The danger of passing on communicable diseases is minimal when using a common cup if it is turned and wiped between each use. If your congregation balks at drinking from a common cup, serve communion by *intinction.* Break off a piece of bread and give it to the communicant, who then dips the bread into the cup and consumes both bread and juice together.
3. See *In the Breaking of the Bread Is Wholeness* (West Lafayette: The Center for Contemporary Celebration, 1977), p. 27.

Chapter 11

1. See Sharon Neufer Emswiler and Tom Neufer Emswiler, *It's Your Wedding: A Practical Guide to Planning Contemporary Ceremonies* (Waco, Tex.: Creative Resources, 1975).
2. *The Healing Light,* rev. ed. (Plainfield, N.J.: Logos International, 1972).
3. *The Gift of Healing* (New York: Harper & Row, 1965).
4. *Healing and Christianity* (New York: Harper & Row, 1973).

Chapter 12

1. Tom Neufer Emswiler and Sharon Neufer Emswiler, eds., *Sisters and Brothers, Sing!* (Normal, Ill.: The Wesley Foundation, 1977).
2. (Paraphrase by Sharon and Tom Neufer Emswiler, addition based on a reading done by Charles E. Erb and Rebecca S. Erb at the Ecumenical Clergy Couples Consultation in Mason, Ohio, October, 1978.)
3. "The Empty Space" is written by Tom Neufer Emswiler and may be performed in worship services without additional permission.
4. From Sharon Neufer Emswiler and Tom Neufer Emswiler, *Women and Worship: A Guide to Non-Sexist Hymns, Prayers, and Liturgies* (New York: Harper & Row, 1974), p. 85.
5. Words and music by Marita Brake, Box 149, Danvers, Illinois, 61732. Used by permission.
6. From Tom Neufer Emswiler and Sharon Neufer Emswiler, eds., *Sisters and Brothers, Sing!,* p. 188. Based on a poem by Barbara A. Clayton; used by permission.

7. Ibid., p. 175.
8. Ibid., p. 181.
9. (Ramsey, N.J.: Paulist Press, 1978).
10. Dennis C. Benson and Stan J. Steward, *The Ministry of the Child* (Nashville: Abingdon, 1978), p. 29.
11. Ibid., p. 48.
12. Ibid., pp. 50–51.
13. Tom Neufer Emswiler and Sharon Neufer Emswiler, eds., *Sisters and Brothers, Sing!,* p. 175.
14. Dedicated to Charlotte Gurtner, who demonstrated the fruits of the Spirit again and again in her work on the Illinois State University Board.
15. Tom Neufer Emswiler and Sharon Neufer Emswiler, eds., *Sisters and Brothers, Sing!,* p. 175.
16. Sharon Neufer Emswiler and Tom Neufer Emswiler, *Women and Worship,* pp. 61–62.
17. Tom Neufer Emswiler and Sharon Neufer Emswiler, *Sisters and Brothers, Sing!,* p. 179.
18. (New York: Harper & Row, 1957, 1973).

Related Books

General books on worship

Micks, Marianne H. *The Future Present.* New York: Seabury, 1970.
Morse, Kenneth. *Move in Our Midst.* Brethren Press, 1977.
Randolph, David James. *God's Party.* Nashville: Abingdon, 1975.
Rivers, Clarence Jos. *Soulful Worship.* Cincinnati: Simuli, Inc., 1974.
———. *The Spirit in Worship.* Cincinnati: Simuli, Inc., 1979.
White, James F. *Christian Worship in Transition.* Nashville: Abingdon, 1976.
———. *New Forms of Worship.* Nashville: Abingdon, 1971.
———. *Introduction to Christian Worship.* Nashville: Abingdon, 1980.
Willimon, William H. *Worship as Pastoral Care.* Nashville: Abingdon, 1979.

Books reflecting feminist concerns in worship

Crotwell, Helen Gray. *Women and the Word—Sermons.* Philadelphia: Fortress, 1978.
Emswiler, Sharon Neufer, and Emswiler, Tom Neufer. *Women and Worship.* New York: Harper & Row, 1974.
Haugerud, Joann. *The Word for Us.* Seattle, Wash.: Coalition on Women and Religion, 1977.
Russell, Letty M., ed. *The Liberating Word.* Philadelphia: Westminster, 1976.
Swidler, Arlene, ed. *Sistercelebrations.* Philadelphia: Fortress, 1974.

Books reflecting other particular concerns of worship: the arts, children's liturgies, ethnic worship

Adams, Doug. *Congregational Dancing in Christian Worship.* Austin: The Sharing Co., 1971.

Ortegel, Sister Adelaide. *Banners and Such.* West Lafayette, Ind.: The Center for Contemporary Celebration, 1976.

————. *A Dancing People.* West Lafayette, Ind.: The Center for Contemporary Celebration, 1976.

Schneider, Kent E. *The Creative Musician in the Church.* West Lafayette, Ind.: The Center for Contemporary Celebration, 1976.

Schneider, Kent E., and Ortegel, Sister Adelaide. *Light—A Language of Celebration.* West Lafayette, Ind.: The Center for Contemporary Celebration, 1973.

Sloyan, Virginia, ed. *Signs, Songs and Stories—Another Look at Children's Liturgies.* Washington, D.C.: The Liturgical Conference, 1974.

Sloyan, Virginia, and Huck, Gabe, eds. *Children's Liturgies.* Washington, D.C.: The Liturgical Conference, 1970.

Sola, Carla De. *The Spirit Moves—A Handbook of Dance and Prayer.* Washington, D.C.: The Liturgical Conference, 1977.

This Far by Faith—American Black Worship and Its African Roots. Washington, D.C.: The Liturgical Conference, 1976.

Hymnals

Emswiler, Tom Neufer, and Emswiler, Sharon Neufer, eds. *Sisters and Brothers, Sing!* Normal, Ill.: The Wesley Foundation, 1977. Available from The Wesley Foundation, 211 North School Street, Normal, Illinois 61761. $4.00 postpaid.

Emswiler, Tom Neufer, and Emswiler, Sharon Neufer, eds. *Put On Your Party Clothes.* Normal, Ill.: The Wesley Foundation, 1977. Available from The Wesley Foundation, address above. $2.50 postpaid.

The Ecumenical Women's Center, ed. *Because We Are One People.* Chicago: The Ecumenical Women's Center, 1974. Available from The Ecumenical Women's Center, 1653 W. School Street, Chicago, Illinois 60657.